CHARL█

A█
TO THE C█

CHARLES CAMERON
ARCHITECT
TO THE COURT OF RUSSIA

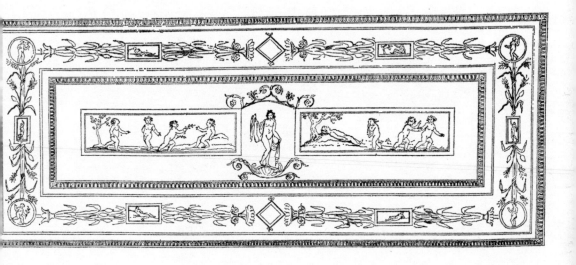

ISOBEL RAE

ELEK BOOKS
LONDON

ISBN 0 236 15423 0

Published by
ELEK BOOKS LIMITED
54–58 Caledonian Road,
London, N.1

Printed in Great Britain
at the St Ann's Press,
Park Road, Altrincham

Contents

List of Plates

32 Section through an unidentified country house designed by Cameron. *State Hermitage Museum, Leningrad.*

War damage in the Green Dining Room and tourists in the Cameron Gallery, Tsarskoe Selo. *Photos: Victor Kennett and Society for Cultural Relations with the USSR*

Endpapers

Elevation of the mirror wall of the Jasper Study of the Agate Pavilion, Tsarskoe Selo. *State Hermitage Museum, Leningrad*

Title page and half titles

Decorative devices from one of the ceilings of the Baths of Titus as shown in *The Baths of the Romans.*

Acknowledgements

I owe grateful thanks to all the archivists and librarians and their staffs who so kindly helped me in my search for the documents without which this book could not have been written; documents which were found in the Public Record Office, Guildhall Library, Corporation of London Archives, Greater London Record Office, Archives of the Westminster City Libraries and H.M. General Register House, Edinburgh.

I am indebted to Sir John Clerk for permission to quote from the Penicuik Papers; to the Earl of Seafield for permission to quote from the Seafield Papers; to the Carpenters' Company and Drummonds Branch, Royal Bank of Scotland Ltd, for permission to quote from their records; to Miss Armet for information about the Bute Archives, and to the Royal Institute of British Architects for permission to quote from a letter in the correspondence files in their library.

I have to thank the authors and publishers who permitted me to use copyright material: John Murray (Publishers) Ltd (*Robert Adam and his Circle* by John Fleming); Faber & Faber Ltd (*Palmyra of the North* by Christopher Marsden); the *R.I.B.A. Journal; The Architectural Review;* and Thames & Hudson Ltd (*A Concise History of Russian Art* by Mrs Talbot Rice). I have also to thank Mrs Talbot Rice, Dr A. A. Tait and the Arts Council of Great Britain for allowing me to quote from the Catalogue of the Cameron Exhibition, 1967–68. I am grateful to Miss Alison Kelly, not only for her book, *Decorative Wedgwood*, but for the help she gave me on the subject.

I must thank, too, the National Library of Scotland, the London Library, the British Museum and the Victoria and Albert Museum for answering so readily all my demands upon them for books for reference, and all those, such as the Novosti Press Agency who helped me to collect pictures for illustrations to this book.

For help and encouragement at the beginning of my search for the elusive Charles Cameron I have to thank Colonel Donald Cameron of Lochiel and, in the USSR, Miss Arenkova, Museum of Architecture, Moscow.

I.R.

Author's Note. In order to avoid confusion the eighteenth-century names, St Petersburg and Tsarskoe Selo, have been used throughout, instead of Leningrad and Pushkin.

I
THE ADVENTURER

I

Scotland

Lady Craven, that tireless traveller, who later became the Margravine of Anspach, describes in her *Memoirs* her introduction to St Petersburg in 1782:

> On my arrival at this city I was presented to the Empress Catherine, who graciously sent me word that she would receive me at the Hermitage previously to the day which had been fixed for my reception at Court. Nothing could be more dignified than the Empress upon her entrance into the drawing-room: her countenance was expressive of good humour, and her politeness and attention to me very great. One of her first inquiries was, if I were not a Scotchwoman: this question arose from some one having informed her that I was not English.

Lady Craven was, in fact, an Englishwoman, but the story not only gives a good idea of atmosphere of the court of Catherine the Great, but reveals that the Empress could appreciate the difference between the inhabitants of North and South Britain and was well acquainted with the Scots.

Scots, indeed, had long been made welcome at the Russian court. Peter the Great was attended by a Scottish doctor, Dr Erskine, a cousin of the Earl of Mar, who roused in his royal patient some sympathy for the Jacobite cause. The Empress Elizabeth, Peter's daughter, had as her first physician Dr James Mounsey from Lochmaben, Dumfriesshire. Catherine carried on the tradition by making Dr John Rogerson, another Dumfriesshire man, her Court Physician, while in her navy two Scotsmen, Admiral Elphinston and his junior, the future Grand Admiral Sir Samuel Greig of Inverkeithing, won for her a famous victory over the Turks at Chesme Bay in 1769. Ten years later she was delighted to welcome to St Petersburg another Scot, the architect Charles Cameron, the subject of this biography.

The medical men all came from the Scottish Lowlands; Cameron, as his name implies, was a Highlander; he was also, so he told the Empress, a Jacobite. A letter of hers, written shortly after his arrival, described him as 'Scottish by nationality, Jacobite by persuasion, great designer trained in the antique manner'.[1] This set him somewhat apart, for here was a young man nobly suffering for his political beliefs, a follower of a lost cause, in voluntary exile from his native land. The effect was heightened in a subsequent letter when Catherine expanded the statement, giving the further information that Cameron had been 'brought up in the Pretender's household in Rome and was a nephew of Miss Jenny Cameron'—consequently he was of good family and gentle birth.

Miss Jenny Cameron of Glendessary, whom Charles Cameron claimed as his aunt, was the granddaughter of Sir Ewen Cameron of Lochiel, a famous Chief of the Clan Cameron, and thus a cousin of 'Gentle' Lochiel, Chief at the time of the 1745 Rebellion. She was then between forty and fifty years of age, and was acting as guardian to her young nephew Donald Cameron; as his representative she rode to Glenfinnan at the head of two hundred and fifty clansmen, bringing with her also a gift of cattle for the Jacobite army. After watching the raising of Prince Charles' standard she left Glenfinnan with the other spectators, and it is stated on good authority that she never met the Prince 'but in public when he had his Court in Edinburgh'.

Miss Jenny Cameron did no more than her duty. She must, however, have been quite a memorable figure that day at Glenfinnan, and, when the story filtered south, the Hanoverian hacks of Grub Street saw that they could make something out of it, to denigrate the Prince and assist their anti-Jacobite propaganda. For this purpose the simple tale had to be embroidered: first of all the London reports declared that the young and beautiful Miss Jenny Cameron had been presented to the Prince at Glenfinnan, that he had escorted her to his tent, and that thereafter she followed him to Edinburgh at the head of her troop.

Not content with this pack of lies, the scribes were emboldened to continue their work. In 1746 three pamphlets appeared, each referred to Miss Jenny as the 'Reputed Mistress' of the Pretender's eldest son, and recounted 'her gallantries in Scotland and France' and other adventures in *Fanny Hill* style, culminating in her capture after Culloden (Plate 1).

No serious reader should have believed this nonsense. Two of the pamphlets were anonymous, and the name of the author of the third has been proved to be fictitious. Nevertheless the harm had been done, the *Memoirs of Miss Jenny Cameron* spread far and wide, a German edition appearing in 1747. Nor was that all; in London in 1746 a pantomime—music by Dr Arne— was staged at Drury Lane, *Harlequin Incendiary or Columbine Cameron*. The principal personages were the Pope, the Devil, the Pretender and Jenny Cameron, whose part was taken by the celebrated actress, Kitty Clive.

Miss Jenny Cameron of Glendessary died in 1772, after a wholly blameless life, but tales of her close connection with the Young Pretender had reached all parts of Europe, including Russia. When Charles Cameron mentioned his aunt Jenny, the Empress Catherine would have recalled immediately the lady and her story—and her kinship with Lochiel.

Miss JENNY CAMERON, the Young Pretender's DIANA.

Jenny, the bold Amazon of the North!   With step intreped marches thro' the Snow:
With high Encomiums Fame proclaims her Worth: Faces the Frost, & mounts the bleaky Brow:
In Bloom of Youth She gave to Love her Charms: The hardy Highlander, enur'd to Cold,
By Age matur'd, she courts the Din of Arms.   Admires her Courage, & becomes more bold:
Zealous for Charles she treads y' rough Campaign, Thy Spirit, Jenny, had deserv'd applause,
And feels the Shiv'ring Winds without a Pain: Hadst thou engag'd in George's nobler Cause.

Publish'd according to Act of Parliament, 1746.

1 Fictitious portrait of Miss Jenny Cameron from a
satirical pamphlet published in 1746.

2 Detail of *Piccadilly Looking West* by James Miller,
showing the end of White Horse Street, *c.* 1775.

3 Detail of a print showing the Fleet Prison at the end
of the eighteenth century.

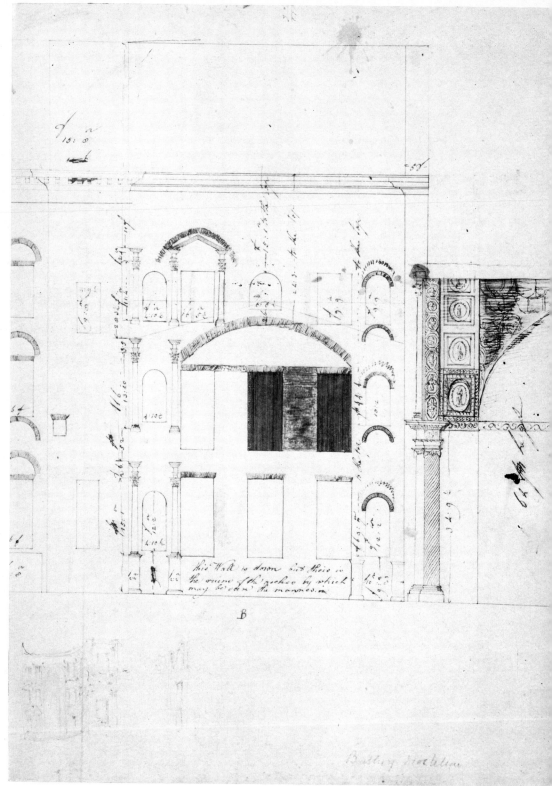

4 Pen and ink study by Cameron of the Baths of
Diocletian (which later formed the basis for a plate in
The Baths of the Romans), showing his early interest
in decoration as well as accurate measurements.

I L
FORESTIERE ISTRUITO
DELLE COSE PIU' RARE
DI ARCHITETTURA,
E di alcune Pitture
DELLA CITTA' DI VICENZA
D I A L O G O
DI OTTAVIO BERTOTTI SCAMOZZI
DEDICATO
AL NOB. SIG. MARCHESE
MARIO CAPRA.

IN VICENZA MDCCLXI.
∽ ✱✱ ∽ ✱✱ ∽ ✱✱ ∽ ✱✱ ∽
Nella Stamperia di GIOVAMBATTISTA VENDRAMINI MOSCA.
CON LICENZA DE' SUPERIORI.

Charles Cameron

5 The title page of Cameron's own first edition copy
of Scamozzi's account of the classical and Palladian
buildings in Vicenza.

6 The frontispiece and the dedication to Lord Bute in *The Baths of the Romans* 1772.

7   The supposed portrait of Charles Cameron by Robert Hunter, 1771, and the authentic one by A. O. Orlovsky, 1809.

8 Portrait of Catherine the Great by M. Shibanov, 1787,
showing her in travelling dress for her journey to the Crimea.

II

London and Rome

'Scottish by nationality, Jacobite by persuasion . . . brought up in the Pretender's household at Rome . . . nephew of Miss Jenny Cameron'. This is what Cameron told the Empress Catherine about himself and this is what she believed—but the truth, as revealed in the records of London in the cold light of the twentieth century, is very different.

Charles Cameron could never have been the nephew of Miss Jenny Cameron, the true Miss Jenny Cameron of Glendessary, since she had only one Cameron nephew, Donald, the son of her brother, Captain Allan Cameron. The old apprenticeship books of the Carpenters' Company of London reveal that Charles Cameron, the future architect, was actually the son of one Walter Cameron, who gave the name of *his* father as 'Archibald Cameron, late of Edinburgh. Gent & decsd'. As there is no mention of any of these men in the family tree of the Camerons of Lochiel, the claim of kinship with his Chief—and the relationship would have been quite close had Charles really been the nephew of Miss Jenny Cameron—was somewhat presumptuous.

In 1740 when Charles' father, Walter Cameron, first emerges from the shadows, it is as a citizen of London. On 6 May of that year, after an apprenticeship to Nicholas Blick, he was made free of the Carpenters' Company 'on the testimony of John Boote, Citizen and Joiner'.[1]

The Carpenters' Company has a long and illustrious history with a Charter dating from the fifteenth century, and although by the beginning of the eighteenth century it had lost some of its power and its monopoly of work in the City, it still provided an excellent training for its members. In those days a carpenter was also a builder; a Master Carpenter had to know all the principles of construction, sometimes receiving the title of 'master-builder', and Walter Cameron made a shrewd choice when he apprenticed himself to Nicholas Blick. Blick became a Liveryman of the Company in 1718 and soon began to take leases of building sites north of Piccadilly where London was rapidly expanding. Curzon Street was first known as Blick Street, when in 1715 Sir Nathaniel Curzon let part of his land (now part of Curzon Street and Stratton Street) on a long building lease to 'Nicholas Blick of St Martin's parish'.

The age of the speculative builder had arrived. By 1763 'Mr Mortimer', who wrote a directory of London *The Universal Director*, observed:

> Of later years Masters of House Carpentry have assumed the name of Builders because they make an estimate of the total expense of a house and contract for the whole of the amount of their estimate; so that they take upon themselves the providing of all materials, and employ their own Masons, Plumbers, Smiths, etc, whereas formerly it was the custom for gentlemen and merchants to apply to the several masters in each branch, and to employ them in executing their plans; this, indeed, is sometimes the case at present, but very rarely, particularly with regard to houses, whole streets having lately been erected by Builders.

In this Walter Cameron was a good pupil of his master, Nicholas Blick. It was not by chance that, in 1740, when he was able to set up on his own, he chose to live on the eastern edge of the development area, in Bolton Street, which had for some time held the record as 'the last built up street before the open country of Knightsbridge'. Very soon Walter Cameron began to buy and sell leases in Mayfair. In 1743 he was assigning to one John Drake 'for the remainder of a term of four score years . . . a parcel or piece of land in a field called the Stone Bridge field which doth abutt east on a plot of garden ground in the tenure of the Rt. Hon. the Earl of Cardigan, and on a Brook running by the said field north and south on the highway leading from Piccadilly to Knightsbridge.[2] There were similar transactions in 1743 and 1756, the land then being in 'Hamilton Street', and this was only the beginning.

The house in which Walter Cameron lived in Bolton Street is unknown, as the houses were not then numbered, but the rate-collector's returns show that it had an assessed rental of £12, and the poor rate, varying from fourpence to sevenpence in the pound, was duly paid until 1747 when the word 'Gone' appears beside his name. He had not gone very far, only round the corner to Portugal Row, to a house with the same assessed rental, £12; but, by the time he left it in 1760, the rates had risen to 12s 6d (10s for the poor; 1s 8d for scavenger; 10d for the highway). This could not have been the reason for his departure because five years later, in 1765, he moved on to White Horse Street (Plate 2), where his house was assessed at £20 and the rates amounted to 35s.[3] This was to be his home for the next ten years; it must have suited him admirably since here he had a lease of the land, and the site was large enough for him to erect on it his workshop and yards as well as some new houses.[4]

It seems likely that his son, Charles, was born in Bolton Street, probably in 1743. Records of the birth are lacking, but as Charles Cameron was apprenticed to his father in the year 1760,[5] and as it was customary in the Carpenters' Company to end the seven-year apprenticeship at the age of twenty-four, 1743 seems to be about the correct date, making Charles a lad of seventeen when he was 'bound' to his father. This was done, as between father and son, for no charge, though Walter Cameron had been permitted to charge twelve guineas 'consideration money' when he took his first apprentice 'John Reed, son of John Reed of the Parish of St George, Hanover Square' on 6 May 1740, the day that he himself became a freeman.

However ardently Charles Cameron in his later years was to proclaim himself a Jacobite, the household in which he was brought up was absolutely loyal to King George. Walter Cameron lived securely in Bolton Street through the troublous days of the Rebellion of the 'Forty-Five, and when it was all over he was still there, paying his rates regularly. Moreover he was still a member of the Carpenters' Company whose loyalty was unquestioned; he could have been one of those anonymous men whom the Company had to send out, according to its records, 'in the Traine Bands occasioned by the Rebells in Scotland'. His political sympathies were revealed in the Westminster by-election of 1749 when he did not give his vote to the Tory candidate, Sir George Vandeput, but to the Whig, Granville Leveson Gower, Viscount Trentham (later 1st Marquis of Stafford), a lord of the Admiralty in Pelham's administration.[6]

There was certainly no exile for Walter Cameron, no residence at the Court of the Pretender for his son, who, in fact, lived in the parental home in White Horse Street until he was a man of over thirty. Indeed Charles Cameron appears to have been lucky in being born into a well-to-do family in a relatively affluent society, where it was easy for him, with his father's workshop on the spot, to pick up the basic principles of his profession without ever leaving Mayfair. From the practical point of view he must in this way have obtained an extraordinarily good grounding in the planning and construction of buildings, but what sort of orthodox schooling he received, and what school, if any, he attended, it seems impossible to discover. Somewhere and somehow, as his book *The Baths of the Romans* shows, he became an extremely well-read man and a good classical scholar with a more than adequate knowledge of the French language. Here again he was lucky, because in the circles in which his father moved all the best books on architectural subjects were available. The eighteenth-century builders who were responsible for the new streets of Mayfair were speculative builders, but not jerry builders; they were intelligent men who knew their job and were interested in it. Recent research into conditions in the Cork Street and Savile Row area during this period of expansion has shown that:

> Of the thirty-eight tradesmen-lessees, some fourteen subscribed to the architectural publications of Leoni, Gibbs, Kent or Ware, although none had subscribed to the expensive volumes of Campbell's *Vitruvius Britannicus*.[7]

Young Charles Cameron kept up this tradition and improved upon it when, in 1771, he became a subscriber to the fifth volume of *Vitruvius Britannicus*, signing himself 'Charles Cameron, architect'.[8]

One book *The Complete Body of Architecture* (1756) must have been in the hands of almost every Carpenter, since its author was the architect Isaac Ware, Master of the Carpenters' Company from 1763 until his death in 1766, a man of humble origins who had made good. It was a compendium of architectural knowledge and became an invaluable text-book; almost every Carpenter studied it, but not every young apprentice had the benefit, as Cameron had, of personal tuition from the author. In an important letter written later to Henry Holland, Samuel Pepys Cockerell states that 'Cameron was bred with Ware'.[9] At first glance the writer might seem to be mistaken, Cameron having been apprenticed to his father and not to Ware, but recent research has made the meaning clear; a copy of Cameron's *Proposals*[10] for publishing his book on the Baths of the Romans by subscription has now been found among the Penicuik Papers in the Register House, Edinburgh, and in this pamphlet he definitely stated that he 'studied under him (Ware) for some time'. It is possible that Isaac Ware and Walter Cameron, both Carpenters, had been friends ever since Walter Cameron gained the freedom of the Company, and that it was through friendship that Ware first took a hand in the boy's education; but he must soon have recognised his talent, and chosen him to help with the engravings for a new edition of the late Lord Burlington's *Fabbriche Antiche* which he was preparing.

Lord Burlington (1694–1753) shared with the architect Colen Campbell (the compiler of *Vitruvius Britannicus*, a collection of engravings of 'classical' British buildings from the previous century and contemporary times) the responsibility for the popularisation of 'Palladianism' in Britain. The work of Palladio, the great sixteenth-century Italian architect, had, it is true, influenced Inigo Jones. However, it was Lord Burlington who made gentlemen builders more aware of Palladio's style and succeeded in impressing it more permanently upon British architecture, especially upon the country houses of the nation, which henceforward developed classical lines and portico fronts consonant with the traditions of ancient Rome and Palladio's own theories of proportion, as stated in his *Four Books of Architecture*. Burlington was a rich man; he was able to go to Italy not once, but twice, and his second visit in 1719 was the more important, both for Architecture and for Charles Cameron. Then it was that he went to Vicenza, where he saw Palladio's villas and bought many of Palladio's drawings of the ruins of the Imperial Baths of Rome. The results of this visit were seen on his return to London: in 1725 he built Chiswick House, that charming, if miniature experiment in Palladianism, and in 1730 he published his *Fabbriche Antiche*, a book containing engravings from his collection of Palladio's drawings, the book which Isaac Ware had hoped to re-issue.

Since Palladio had left many drawings unfinished when he died in 1580, it became a pastime with succeeding generations of architects to 'correct' them. In 1765 Isaac Ware, however, appears to have been preparing a straightforward second edition of Burlington's book, which by then was out of print. Ware was too busy and successful an architect to have time to spare for the niceties of 'correction'; he had built Chesterfield House in London for Lord Chesterfield, and Wrotham Park for Admiral Byng, and all through his life he was employed at H.M. Board of Works where, at his death, he held the positions of secretary, clerk itinerant and clerk of works.

Isaac Ware died on 5 January 1766, a year that seems to have been one of decision for Charles Cameron, perhaps by coincidence. It should have been his last year as an apprentice, but he did not finish his apprenticeship, and so was never admitted to the freedom of the Carpenters' Company. This need not necessarily be held against him. There was a building boom at the end of the Seven Years' War, and many other young apprentices were weighing up the situation. With so much building going on in London beyond the City bounds where the Company had no authority, it was hardly worth paying the requisite six guineas for their freedom, and to continue the work of an apprentice which carried with it little or no pay.

But Charles Cameron may have had other reasons, and Isaac Ware, Master of the Carpenters' Company, may not have looked with such a kindly eye on his young assistant at the end of his life. In the previously quoted letter to Henry Holland, Cockerell referred also to 'some stories about Ware's daughter' and Cameron, implying that these were far from creditable to him; but details of the scandal were not given. Ware's daughters have remained shadowy figures. They were the children of his second wife and in his Will, dated 8 February 1765, he remembered them and left the residue of his personal estate 'to my daughter Mary, now living with me and who was the youngest born of my last wife, formerly Mary Bolton . . . and to my daughter Charlotte, now also living with me, and who was the eldest born of my said last wife, the sum of four hundred pounds'. Whether the 'stories' about Charles Cameron and Ware's daughter referred to Mary or to Charlotte, or, assuming the legal grammar to be correct, to a third daughter no longer living, will probably never be known.

Charles Cameron was not mentioned in Ware's will, but somehow the plates for the projected book came into his possession. By the end of the year he must have decided that he would abandon everything else, finish engraving the plates, and then, making use of some, would publish not a reprint of Lord Burlington's book but his own original work on the Imperial Baths of Rome. In March 1767 he published a preliminary advertisement for subscribers to a volume on the 'Thermae of the Roman Emperors', and a few months later he was showing six engravings at the Free Society of Artists' exhibition in Pall Mall: 'proof prints of ancient Thermae, intended for the work which is publishing' and one engraving of an antique vase. He gave his address as 'next door to Lord Egremont's, Piccadilly' (his home address, as his father's land in White Horse Street adjoined Egremont House).

Cameron had not wasted much time, and this acceptance of his prints by the Free Society may have appeared to him as the first step to fame. The Free Society was an offshoot of the Royal Society of Arts and in 1767 rented for its exhibition the 'Great New Room in Pall Mall, later Mr Lambe's'. Mr Lambe had been an auctioneer, and the premises, at the south-east end of Pall Mall, had a top room with glass skylights where the pictures could be shown to advantage, and probably to a fashionable throng, since the Royal Academy of Arts was not founded until the following year. Cameron therefore had a certain amount of luck in this first presentation of his work to the public; not that it aroused any public attention, and indeed, if the engraving of the antique vase bore any resemblance to his later etching of 'an ornamented jug designed for the Duke of Mantua by Giulio Romano', now in the British Museum, it would have given little indication of budding genius.

Obviously the next step was to go to Rome to inspect and measure the actual Baths, because Cameron, like others before him, intended to 'verify and correct' Palladio's plans. At this time the tremendous concentration by all architects on the correct measurements of the Imperial Baths was due in the first place to a misconception by the great Palladio himself. Before the development of modern archaeological excavation, only the larger buildings, temples and baths which had survived above the ground were visible, and so Palladio erroneously assumed that the domestic dwellings of ancient Rome, which had not survived, were on a similar scale. This resulted in English country house architecture in the mid-eighteenth century being designed by his followers in the grandiose manner of Roman temples and baths, with vast pillared porticoes and Pantheon-like domes—the style which was introduced into the U.S.A. by Jefferson, and taken to Russia by Cameron.

It cost a considerable amount of money to make the 'Grand Tour' to Italy in the eighteenth century, when it was an extremely fashionable thing to do. In 1767 Cameron ought to have been earning his living as a carpenter or builder, had he finished his apprenticeship as his father intended, and it must have been a disappointment for Walter Cameron to find that his son was, instead, an unemployed architect. Nevertheless he must have provided the funds which enabled Charles to go to Rome, as no wealthy patron appears to have been involved. That Charles Cameron was actually in Rome in the following year is indisputable. Hayward's *List of British Artists in Rome in 1768* gives his name, 'Mr Cammeron—architect'.

Life in Rome in 1768 had changed little since Robert Adam was there twelve years before, hardly at all since Boswell's visit in 1765. There were many English milords to be found, and the British tourists in general tended to take lodgings near the Piazza di Spagna and to spend many pleasant hours gossiping in the coffee houses. In order to see the sights and to obtain the necessary introductions, they put themselves into the hands of learned guides or 'antiquaries', often artists themselves, many of whom happened to be Scots.

Cameron could not afford to waste his time on social pleasures, like some of his fellow tourists, if he were to complete the book he had in mind. Soon, so he tells us in that book, he obtained permission from Pope Clement XIII to undertake excavations

> in such places as might assist me in my design of illustrating the Baths. I chose for my chief researches those of Titus in preference to the rest, as being situated on the declivity of a hill and consequently more easy of access.

Not that anything was really easy. Cameron found to his cost that

> the chambers in the lower, or ground floor of the Baths are in general so choaked up with earth that one cannot without great labour and difficulty examine the structure of them.

It was even more difficult to gain access to a room he marked in his plan as 'A', 'where the ornaments of the ceiling were very fresh'. Cameron described his struggles here:

> I was obliged to cut a hole through the wall (B) and to let myself down by a rope and afterwards to creep through a hole in the wall (O) upon my hands and knees. It was nearly full of earth to the ceiling.

In another room he found 'a conduit of water', and in another

> upon the fascia arch little figures two inches high, made of a composition which very much resembles red putty, but upon touching, it crumbles into powder. The ground was painted green.

There was also a staircase built of brick, 'in the same manner as those of Diocletian's Baths'. More practical was his discovery of an antique painting showing the 'disposition of the apartments of the Baths', and the method of heating the water.

It may have been during this visit to Rome that Cameron began to profess Jacobite sympathies. It was not very dangerous to do so twenty-two years after Culloden; even earlier some loyal Whigs had been known to square their consciences when they arrived in Rome and discovered that the best 'antiquaries' were either confessed Jacobites, or suspected of Jacobite leanings. One of the most famous and popular of these men was the Abbé Peter Grant, now sixty years old, a Gaelic speaker from Glenlivet, who for the past thirty years had held the post of Roman Agent for the Scottish Catholic Mission, and knew everybody who was anybody in Rome. From the ease with which he obtained introductions to the Vatican, he was known as 'il introduttore', and Cameron would have been foolish not to have availed himself of his services. Cameron had his audience of the Pope, but he arrived in Rome too late to be presented to the Old Pretender at his Court at the Palazzo Muti in the Piazza de San' Apostoli, reputedly the scene of his own upbringing. Prince James Francis Edward Stuart had died on 1 January 1766, at the age of seventy-eight.

Outside Rome the ubiquitous Abbé Grant could also be of assistance in organising visits to Naples, Herculaneum and Pompeii, and Cameron probably did ask Grant to arrange this tour. Pompeii then had the charm of novelty, for whereas Herculaneum had been opened up in 1713, systematic excavation did not begin at Pompeii until 1763. Sir William Hamilton, British envoy at Naples, was busy acquiring his collection of antique vases and other treasures from the ruins, and had, during the previous two years, 1766–67, published four volumes with engravings of them—his *Collection of Etruscan, Greek and Roman Antiquities.* These had a considerable influence on Josiah Wedgwood, and perhaps also on Charles Cameron. Cameron, as his later work revealed, was much influenced by the Pompeian style of decoration.

Of the many artists in Rome in the year 1768, the only one who played any part in Cameron's later life in Russia was a Frenchman, Charles Louis Clérisseau, draughtsman, architect and prolific painter of ruins. He was a strange character; Falconet referred to him as 'a turbulent man' and at this period of his life—he was forty-seven—he had quarrelled with almost everybody except Robert Adam. Soon after he left Scotland in 1754 Robert Adam met him in Florence, where Clérisseau had just parted in anger from William Chambers. Realising his worth, Adam invited the Frenchman to Rome, to live there, all expenses paid, as his 'antiquarian' and teacher of perspective and drawing. As this arrangement gave Clérisseau ample opportunity for painting the pictures he needed to provide himself with an income and moreover, as Robert Adam was a good pupil and worked hard under his tuition, Clérisseau settled down and remained with him all the time he was in Italy. Together they toured the sights of Rome, sketching and working in minute detail on Hadrian's Villa and the Baths of Diocletian and Caracalla when Adam thought of writing a book about them. Many of Adam's sketches are lost, but many of Clérisseau's remain, all illustrating his delicate and accurate handling of his subjects. After two years they decided to give the same close scrutiny to the remains of Diocletian's palace at Spalato (Split) in Dalmatia.

Robert Adam always had a keen eye to his own advancement. He knew how much he owed to Clérisseau and his knowledge of classical and Renaissance art; he declared that Clérisseau had 'all the knacks so necessary to us architects' and he was determined that these knacks should not be revealed to pupils outside the Adam family. Therefore, when he left Italy in 1757 to return to England, Robert Adam offered Clérisseau a retaining fee of £100 a year to await the arrival of his brother James and to travel with him in the same capacity of escort and tutor, meanwhile supervising in Rome the engraving of the plates for Robert's book *The Ruins of the Palace of the Emperor Diocletian at Spalatro*, published in 1764.

When in 1768 Charles Cameron arrived in Rome James Adam had come and gone, the *Ruins of Spalatro* had been published, and Robert Adam was established in London as an architect with a growing reputation, one who had mastered all the 'knacks'. Thus Clérisseau, although still the Adams' *chargé d'affaires* in Rome, would have been free to impart his knowledge to students other than the Adam brothers. His encyclopaedic knowledge of the Baths of Diocletian and Caracalla, where he had worked so carefully with Robert Adam, would have been invaluable to Cameron. When Cameron was to tell Catherine the Great, probably truthfully, that he admired Clérisseau and had a great regard for him, he said nothing about studying with him. Yet, when Cameron's work is compared with that of Clérisseau's other pupils, Robert Adam and Thomas Jefferson, the resemblance is almost too startling to be coincidental.

Within ten years both Clérisseau and Cameron, one after the other, were to find themselves working for the Empress Catherine II, yet neither of them at this time could have foreseen this. Nevertheless, in 1768, St Petersburg would have been much in the minds of architects working in Rome. The strange northern city set on the sand-banks of the river Neva was only sixty years old, and the fame of the new buildings which Peter the Great's successors had added and were adding to it must have been a talking point, since many of them had been designed by Italian architects.

The most important example was Bartolommeo Francesco Rastrelli (known as Rastrelli 'the younger', because his father, an Italian sculptor, had worked in St Petersburg for Peter the Great). He became official architect to Peter's daughter, the Empress Elizabeth, in 1741 and, working in the Baroque style, he built for her the palace of Tsarskoe Selo. In 1762 he had completed his masterpiece, the Winter Palace. Although Rastrelli received no new commissions from Catherine II when she became Empress of All the Russias in 1762, another Italian, Antonio Rinaldi, had, by 1768, finished one palace for her and begun another. The first was the Chinese Palace in the grounds of Oranienbaum, the second an impressive new building which the Empress intended for her favourite, Count Orlov. This was the Marble Palace in St Petersburg; in contradistinction to the customary brick and stucco, it was faced with red granite and grey Siberian marble and it was indeed splendid. News of it could hardly have failed to reach Rome, and there must also have been some talk about the amazing and formidable woman who had now occupied the Russian throne for six years. Some stories may have been received at first hand, since Catherine had already become an art collector and James Byres, the Scot who had acted as 'antiquary' to Edward Gibbon, was commissioned as an art-dealer to buy fine gem-stones for her in Rome.

When Cameron ultimately arrived in St Petersburg, he led Catherine to understand that he had spent 'long years' studying in Rome, yet there is no record of his stay being prolonged into 1769, and indeed it must have been imperative for him to go to London to prepare his book for publication. When he did return to London he was more Roman than the Romans; with a certain amount of affectation his signature had become, temporarily, 'Carolus Cameron'.

III

The Baths of the Romans

In March 1770 Cameron had his final advertisement for the publication by subscription of his projected book 'The Thermae of the Roman Emperors' printed and despatched to his friends and to booksellers in London, Oxford and Cambridge. Subscriptions were to be sent to the author 'next door but one to Egremont House, Piccadilly', and the book was promised by the end of the year. But *The Baths of the Romans*, as the book was ultimately entitled, was apparently not as near completion as the author had thought, or maybe the subscriptions did not come in sufficiently fast, since it was not until the spring of 1772 that it appeared for sale at the advertised price of four guineas.

Once again Cameron had a well-timed exhibition of his engravings, giving himself and his book a little extra publicity in May 1772, when three of his prints were hung at the Society of Artists' exhibition. Cameron might have made contact in Rome with the man who was then the Society's President. A 'Mr Kirby, architect', was also in Rome in 1768 and was surely that Joshua Kirby, Royal Clerk of Works, whose artistic pretensions have been dismissed as the 'slenderest', and he himself as 'totally unfit to act as President of a Society whose members included Reynolds, Gainsborough, Zoffany and Stubbs'.[1] In fact most of these were soon asked by Kirby to resign because they had exhibited at the new and rival Royal Academy.

In 1768 no less than 18,000 visitors had paid one shilling each for admission to the Society of Artists' exhibition, but thereafter the takings fell, as London society followed the Court to the new Royal Academy. Two years later, when James Paine, the architect, became President of the Society, he decided to improve the situation by buying a site on the north side of the Strand on which to build an Academy with exhibition rooms and other accommodation. So it was that Cameron found his prints hung in the best possible conditions: in a 'fine and handsome' building, in the gallery with the 'green distempered walls and chocolate-coloured dado'. In addition there was a grand official opening ceremony on 11 May 1772; the company present was 'noble, select, and respectable', an orchestral musical programme was conducted by Giardini and for the occasion a special ode was composed, the chorus of which, in somewhat pedestrian verse, went as follows:

'Behold the Arts around us bloom
And its muse-devoted Dome
Rivals the works of Athens and Rome'.

And there on the wall, showing the grandeur that was Rome, were Cameron's three prints, all longitudinal or transverse sections of Antoninus' (Caracalla's) baths, all 'restored from the ruins' in the traditional manner. It was the last time that Cameron was to sign himself 'engraver'; thereafter he was, as he has remained, 'Charles Cameron, architect'. His address he gave once more as 'the corner of White Horse Street, Piccadilly'.

In the eighteenth century 'architect' was a self-bestowed title that was won neither by examination nor training, but presumably the men who used it were certain that they were capable of designing sound structures. The word itself seems to have first appeared in the language in the sixteenth century, but it was in the middle of the eighteenth century that it came into general use, when architects themselves proliferated. If the architect had by then become an integral part of the social system and a member of an honourable profession, Charles Cameron had very little to show—not a single building that can be identified—when he appended the word to his name. But he had at least produced a book, and at this period every architect with any pretensions to fame felt the need to publish one. Cameron however was late in the field and could not hope to emulate the standard works of James Gibbs (*Book of Architecture* 1728) nor of Sir William Chambers (*Treatise on Civil Architecture* 1759) nor of his master Isaac Ware, and wisely he chose to write the *Baths of the Romans* in 'antiquarian' style. While working in this *genre* Cameron might have produced something like Robert Adam's *Ruins*, 'different from all other things yet published'. Instead, he went back to the hackneyed subject of the ruins of Rome; but of course, as the recent discovery of his *Proposals* for publishing his book by subscription reveals, he intended from the start to make good use of the engravings of Palladio's unfinished sketches of the Baths, which Ware 'had left imperfect at his death'.

The subject of Cameron's book *The Baths of the Romans* may have lacked novelty, but it has the distinction of being written in two languages. When it appeared in 1772 it was in one volume with one set of prints, but with identical English and French texts. It was 'printed by George Scott, Chancery Lane, and to be had of The Author, next door to Egremont House, Piccadilly' and it had an effusive dedication to Lord Bute.

John Stuart, 3rd Earl of Bute, ranks high among unpopular Prime Ministers. He had a haughty manner; he was a Scot; he was believed to exert undue influence over the Princess of Wales and her son, George III, and so bitterly was he attacked for the Peace of Paris, which he concluded with France in 1763, that two months later he resigned office and retired into private life. Then, being himself a man of substance and having married the heiress daughter of Lady Mary Wortley Montagu, he was able to indulge himself as a patron of the arts, and commissioned Robert Adam to design Luton Hoo, the mansion in Bedfordshire (1766–70) which housed his magnificent paintings and valuable library. He was interested in science, particularly in botany, but his 'darling art' was said to be architecture; therefore *The Baths of the Romans* was a subject likely to attract his interest. Lord Bute was well known, only too well known, for his kindness to his fellow Scots, and his biographer, J. A. Lovat Fraser, quotes Dutens as speaking of 'the secret assistance which he rendered to poverty stricken artists . . . especially those who hailed from his native land'.

Perhaps Bute did secretly help Cameron to defray the cost of printing the *Baths*. The volume is still in the Bute library, but the remaining Bute archives (many were burnt in the fire at his home at Luton Hoo) contain no correspondence about the dedication, nor is there any reference to Cameron. Alternatively there may have been no need for correspondence; the two men could have met in Italy in 1768 when Bute was travelling there incognito as Sir John Stuart. They could have been introduced by their mutual friend the Abbé Grant; while in London Lord Bute and Cameron were quite near neighbours, Bute at Bute House in South Audley Street, and Cameron at White Horse Street.

In whatever way it originated, the dedication to Lord Bute has its rightful place at the beginning of *The Baths of the Romans*, and a handsome dedication it is. The engraving is undoubtedly the finest in the book, the Bute coat of arms being particularly good (Plate 6). It bears the signature of 'C. Hall, 24, Margaret Street, Cavendish Square', that is Charles Hall, then a man of just over fifty, a writing engraver who 'aspired to a higher branch of art and was much employed in engraving portraits, coins, medals and other antiquities'. The text, an equally good specimen of craftsmanship, seems to imply a certain personal contact between Cameron and Lord Bute:

'To the Earl of Bute

My Lord,
    Your Lordship will not be surprised in seeing this volume which contains some of the noblest Remains of Ancient Genius, inscribed to you—for the Arts naturally fly to their Admirers and Friends.
    Their innate Worth and Beauty first recommended and still endear them to you. Upon this Consideration I have presumed to ask your protection for the following Sheets, it being at once the motive and justification of him who is, My Lord, with all possible respect,
                    Your Lordship's
                        Most obedient and very humble servant,
                            Charles Cameron.'

Many of the engravings in the book were taken straight from Burlington's *Fabbriche Antiche*, and Cameron now presented them 'corrected and improved' because they had been left unfinished at Palladio's death. Other engravings are Isaac Ware's, designed for his projected new edition of the *Fabbriche Antiche*. But it has been pointed out that although Cameron in his advertisement for the publication of his book by subscription specifically stated that he intended to 'complete the designs Mr Ware left imperfect at his death' and to give them 'to the public, verified and corrected, with their measures from his own observations', when *The Baths of the Romans* finally appeared in print no mention of any kind was made of Cameron's debt to Ware, nor is there any acknowledgment of the use which he made of his old master's prints. This 'does not throw wholly favourable light on Cameron's character'.[2]

Throughout *The Baths of the Romans* Cameron reveals not only his antiquarian interests but also his very practical ability. He is delighted to reproduce the painting he had discovered in the Baths of Titus of the method employed to heat the water. He quotes the description ('Cambden II p 828') of 'two Roman Hypocausta recently discovered in England' and by some extraordinary calculations, based on two of Piranesi's prints of sections of the Castella of Antoninus, he concludes that the ancient Romans, using upper and lower heating chambers 'could be in no difficulty of heating the greatest bodies of water that their most extensive *Thermae* required':

> Allowing therefore eight cubic ft of warm water as sufficient for one man to bathe in, and that water preserved in a bathing heat in the Labrum half-an-hour, the whole consumption of hot water in this given time for 18,000 people would be 144,000 cubic ft. By this calculation there would be a sufficient quantity of water for three hours, or until five in the evening for 108,000 people.

Cameron was also extremely interested in the method of building the baths and reproduces another Piranesi print to illustrate the details of construction: stone and cement filling in between brick linings; tiles, and incrustation of marble fastened by cramps of bronze to the wall, plain and ornamented stucco on walls, ceilings and vaults; pieces of marble placed upon stucco to make the surface even, etc. On these technicalities he comments with all the knowledge of a trained builder.

The reader of these passages gains confidence in Cameron as an architect. Surely a man who went into such painstaking detail would build sound foundations. Surely his plumbing would be faultless, the hot water ever constant. Could it be that this was in fact the reaction of the Empress Catherine when, some years later, the book reached her hands?

IV

Litigation

Cameron was about thirty years old in 1772, when he published his *Baths of the Romans* and he must have hoped, perhaps expected, that commissions would flow in as a result of it. But apparently nothing happened; the book may have sold well, but there was not even a review in the *Gentleman's Magazine* which, in its *Catalogue of New Publications*, gave no more than the title, under the heading 'scientific books'.

It was fortunate that the young man could continue to live and work under his father's roof where he may, for all we know, have been the anonymous architect of some of the smaller houses then being erected in the new streets of Mayfair.

The only biography in English of Charles Cameron was published in London in 1943, and was translated from the Russian of Georges Loukomski, a former Curator of the palace of Tsarskoe Selo. Professor D. Talbot Rice, in his introduction to the book, suggests that future research might result in the attribution to Cameron of 'some of the vast array of unassigned Georgian buildings of England, or more probably Scotland'. Research, however, has revealed nothing of this, and for three years, until 1775, the next milestone in his life, Cameron simply disappears. One thing that has bedevilled past efforts to read the riddle of his life is that the British have always believed that the Russians must hold the answer, while the Russians have similarly believed the clues to be in British hands; it now appears that the art historians of both countries have been equally ignorant.

Loukomski tries to fill the gap after the *Baths of the Romans* with the suggestion that Cameron was in Dublin in 1773 and had his portrait painted there by the Irish artist Robert Hunter; he goes so far as to use the portrait of a dark, bearded young man dressed in pseudo-Russian costume as the frontispiece to his biography (Plate 7). The history of the picture is quite well known, but no one else has ever claimed that the young man is Charles Cameron. Strickland's *Dictionary of Irish Artists* gives a list of Hunter's known paintings and in it there is no mention of a portrait of Charles Cameron, although there is a description which aptly fits Loukomski's picture:

A Gentleman in blue, Russian costume, standing by a window on which rests an architectural plan. Inscribed R. Hunter pinxit Dublinii 1771.

Somebody must be wrong here, since Loukomski states that the picture is dated 1773, but his evidence to prove the identity of the sitter is, to say the least, doubtful. The 'architectural plan' he assumes to be of the Baths, but even if it were, Cameron was far from having a monopoly of such a subject. Why Cameron, eight years before he went to Russia where he never wore Russian costume, should be shown dressed in these fanciful garments is never satisfactorily explained. Indeed Loukomski's explanations make matters worse: he claims that a bust in the background represents Lord Bute, yet under close examination the likeness is difficult to confirm, and the statement that the words 'Lord Bute's Agent' are on the back of the canvas is hardly helpful because the names of the men whom Bute employed to buy works of art for him in Italy are known and Cameron was not among them.

Both Loukomski and Strickland agree that the picture was sold at Christie's —the Townshend heirlooms sale—in 1904. The purchaser was David Minlore, Esq., in whose possession the portrait was when Loukomski reproduced it in 1943. Now it is in a Moscow Museum, but a more authentic portrait of Cameron, as an old man wearing an English style jacket, is in the Russian State Museum in Leningrad (Plate 7).

The evidence for Cameron's visit to Ireland is tenuous, and how he spent the years from 1772–75 must remain a matter for conjecture. He could equally well have gone to Paris where his book was on sale and thus come into contact with the work of Neo-classical architects like Soufflot. But, in view of his later style, a more reasonable supposition might be that he stayed in London to study interior decoration, where between the years 1772 and 1775 Robert Adam was the acknowledged leader in the field. Although they both lived in Mayfair, it is unlikely that they ever met. Adam had chosen his address in Lower Grosvenor Street for social reasons, 'to blind the world by dazzling their eyesight with vain pomp', and he was not a man who would consort with humbler compatriots in the area.

But if Charles Cameron did not meet Adam, it is probable that Isaac Ware had done so. Mr John Fleming throws out this interesting suggestion in his book *Robert Adam and His Circle*, his idea being that they may have met in the 1750s when Ware went to Scotland to build New Milns (Amiesfield) in Midlothian for the Earl of Wemyss.[1] Mr Fleming adds:

> Though externally one of the most faithful Burlingtonians, Ware relaxed his strict Palladian principles in favour of 'judicious variety' indoors. He would therefore have commended Robert's introduction of rococo 'lightness' inside both Hopetoun and Dumfries House.

So it may be that Cameron, through Ware, had his mind alerted to the 'Adam style' at a much earlier and more impressionable age than might have been expected. Living as he did in London, he had to make only a short journey from Piccadilly to Brentford and Isleworth to see Adam's men actually at work. At Brentford Adam was redecorating and modernising the Earl of Northumberland's Tudor mansion, Syon House, and at Isleworth he was similarly engaged at Osterley Park, then owned by Francis Child of the famous banking family. In both cases the work was well advanced by the time of Isaac Ware's death in 1766, and in the following year Adam was entrusted by Lord Mansfield with the redecoration of his Hampstead home, Kenwood. Even supposing that, despite their proximity to Piccadilly, young Cameron had not the entrée to these places, there still remains Luton Hoo, Bedfordshire where from 1766–70 Adam was making very extensive alterations for Lord Bute. If the dedication of *The Baths of the Romans* to Lord Bute meant anything, Charles Cameron should have been aware of what was going on there.

Charles Cameron was at one with Robert Adam in his admiration of Clérisseau, who in 1771 suddenly appeared in London, brought over from Italy by Adam. In the following year, when Cameron was showing prints at the Society of Artists, Clérisseau had one of his, 'A Bath Composed After the Manner of the Ancients', hung in the Royal Academy exhibition. In 1773 he was submitting plans to the Empress Catherine of Russia for 'a Graeco-Roman house' and, if Cameron heard of this, it could have put ideas into his head; but much was to happen before he found himself in Russia. Within a twelvemonth he applied for the post of district surveyor for the metropolitan area of Middlesex, perhaps under some pressure from his family to find some sort of paying job and settle down. At any rate he showed so little interest in it that he did not appear for the necessary interview; the records briefly state that 'being absent he was not examined'.[2] So that was the end of that.

In 1775 a second edition of *The Baths of the Romans* was published. Today copies of it are scarce, so perhaps it may be the edition of which only fifty copies were said to have been printed. Whereas the first edition had been published by George Scott, Chancery Lane, the new edition was 'printed for S. Leacroft at The Globe, Charing Cross; and J. Matthews, No 18 Strand'. The format of the book remained unchanged; the plates are at the end, the French version of 1772 in the middle, and the English text at the beginning, but the title page bears the date of 1775, and has been considerably altered. The letter-press has been compressed to permit the insertion at the bottom of the page of a print—'Exedra in Titus's Baths'—used as a chapter heading in the original edition, and also significantly perhaps, there is no mention that the book can be obtained 'of the author'. In the light of things to come it could be that this edition was an unauthorised publication.

This year, 1775, was to prove a fateful one for Charles Cameron. In May his father, Walter Cameron, for the first time failed to pay his rates; he was £2 in arrears for his property in White Horse Street, £2 only, yet as he could not meet the bill, his financial position must indeed have been precarious.[3] The causes of this reversal of fortune are obscure—conditions might have been difficult owing to the outbreak of war with the American Colonies—but the results are not. For the next eighteen months the family was involved in almost constant litigation; the story is confused and has to be pieced together from records which are sometimes incomplete and where details are often lacking, records which are spread over London, in the archives of Guildhall, the Public Record Office, the Westminster Public Library and County Hall, but the main outline of events appears to be as follows.

In the early months of 1775 Walter Cameron was involved in what seems to have been his first law-suit. The brief record of the case 'Richard Remnant & John Coleman *v*. Walter Cameron' appears in the King's Bench Entry Books of Judgments,[4] but no more can be discovered about it. A few months later Charles Cameron was himself a defendant in some case about which all details are lacking.[5] Then, a year later, in the Trinity Term 1776, the King's Bench Records reveal that judgment was given against Walter Cameron at the 'suit of Jervois Clarke for £2433-19-0';[6] that is all, but the Middlesex Land Register at County Hall produces indentures between Walter Cameron and 'Jervoise Clarke of the parish of St George, Hanover Square, in the County of Midsx, Esq' in February and April 1776, proving that Cameron was then selling to Clarke the residue of the lease of his property in White Horse Street:

> all that piece or parcel of ground situate and being in Piccadilly aforesaid in the parish of St George, Hanover Square together with the messuage or tenement yards and workshop thereon erected and built and now in the tenure or occupation of the said Walter Cameron. (Feb. 15)[7]

On 26 April 1776 the second indenture between Walter Cameron and Clarke was signed 'being a further charge of the lease mentioned'.[8] Cameron had now left White Horse Street, and Jervoise Clarke may have been anxious about his lease, since the 'parcel of ground' is described in far more detail:

> next adjoining Egremont House 34 ft or thereabouts, and from east to west at rear thereof whereon the workshop stood 33 ft 18 inches or thereabouts and from north to south on the side next White Horse Street 79 ft.

Unfortunately, in the previous June, perhaps pressed by Richard Remnant and John Coleman, Walter Cameron had already mortgaged the property to Mrs Anne Burnell, widow, of Salisbury Court, Fleet Street,[9] and although she, along with Cameron, had signed the transfer to Jervoise Clarke on 15 February 1776, it was made clear in the Indenture of 26 April 1776 that 'all assignments, mortgages and securities' were now 'vested in the said Jervoise Clarke'. What happened in May and June to induce Jervoise Clarke to bring Walter Cameron to court and to obtain such a heavy judgment against him as £2433-19s is not recorded, but it seems reasonable to assume that for some cause, perhaps because of the mortgage, Walter Cameron was unable to keep his bargain and give Jervoise Clarke a valid lease.

Walter Cameron was in a sad plight, and it was to be made worse by the action of his own son who intervened to make his father answer 'a plea of trespass on the case',[10] accusing him—and here the evidence is still extant in the Common Pleas Plea Roll for the Michaelmas Term, 1776—of possessing himself of Charles' property and

> contriving and fraudulently intending craftily and subtilly to deceive and defraud the said Charles Cameron in this behalf hath not yet delivered the said goods and chattels or any of them to the said Charles Cameron although so to do the said Walter Cameron by the said Charles Cameron at Westminster hath been oftentimes requested, but to do this the said Walter Cameron hath hitherto wholly refused and afterwards to wit on the same day and year above at Westminster (22 June 1776) converted and disposed thereof to his own use to the said Charles Cameron his damage £1500 and therefore he brings suit.

As Charles Cameron accused his father of acquiring the property 'by finding' it might have come into his hands when he was clearing out the White Horse Street house, where his son had also resided; but what a find it was! Charles enumerated his lost goods and chattels as

> to wit ten book-cases, twenty busts, twenty Pictures, twenty portrait pictures, five hundred printed books intermixed with prints taken from copper plates, five hundred other printed books, five hundred other books and one thousand other prints of the value of £1500.

The loss was considerable, because it is more than likely that some of these busts and pictures—landscapes and portraits and prints—represented purchases made by Charles when he was in Italy.

Walter Cameron pleaded 'not guilty' to these charges against him and the case went forward for trial by jury at Westminster Hall on 29 November 1776, Sir William de Grey on the bench. The verdict was in favour of Charles:

> Walter Cameron found guilty of the premises within laid to his charge in manner and form as the said Charles hath within complained against him and they assess the damages of the said Charles by reason thereof besides his costs and charges by him laid out and expended about his suit in this behalf to £130 and for his said costs and charges to 40/- . . . also £77 to the said Charles at his request for costs and charges aforesaid by the Court here for Increase adjudged which said Damages in the whole amount to £209.

This was satisfactory for Charles as far as it went, although he must have known that he had not the least chance of ever receiving his money because his father, on 29 August 1776, had been committed to the debtors' prison, the Fleet. 'Detained at the suit of Charles Cameron' states the *List of Prisoners in the Fleet* in 1778, while, in the 1780 list, the reference to Walter Cameron's detention gives the same date of committal, 29 August 1776, but in the column headed 'at whose suit detained' it is stated 'by the King upon an attachment in Common Pleas for not delivering up fifty-six copper plates

35

pursuant to a rule of Court'. This appears to be a consequence of Charles Cameron's intervention with his accusation of 'trespass on the case'; but if, as Samuel Pepys Cockerell believed, the copper plates were those used for the engravings in *The Baths of the Romans*, Charles Cameron had every reason for anger, although the part he played in consigning his own father to the Fleet was not a pretty one and caused him to be held in small esteem by his contemporaries.

Walter Cameron remained a prisoner in the Fleet until June 1780 when, like so many others, he was liberated during the Gordon Riots. He remained at liberty for over two months; then, deciding maybe that life inside the prison was more pleasant for a debtor than that outside, he gave himself up to the authorities on 31 August 1780.[11] The stock form for such surrenders ran as follows:

> I do acknowledge myself to have been a prisoner in the custody of the marshall of the King's Bench Prison, but set at large by the fire on 7th June, and came this day to surrender myself again. As witness my hand this day.

After that no more is heard of Walter Cameron, by then a man of over sixty, and he may have died in the Fleet (Plate 3).

Nor in England is anything more heard of his son, who by 1780 was well established in St Petersburg at the Court of Catherine the Great. What Charles Cameron did between 1776 and 1779 is unknown, but it must have been quite clear to him when the 'Cameron Case' ended as it did, that his unpopularity in London was such that he need not look there for commissions and professional advancement. If his ambition were to be satisfied he must go abroad.

How then did Cameron obtain his introduction to Catherine II? The answer to this question seems most likely to be found in Rome, in the person of her agent, Reiffenstein, Director of the Russian Academy there. The suggestion has been made that Clérisseau brought *The Baths of the Romans* and its author to her notice, but this seems improbable. Later on, after 1779, Clérisseau was in such favour that the Empress bought many drawings from him, but before that a recommendation from him would hardly have carried much weight. His designs for the 'Graeco-Roman house' she had commanded in 1773 were not a success; they were for a building about three times the size she had envisaged, as was his fee, and Falconet, writing to Prince Galitzin about Clérisseau in December 1773, remarked 'He has put Her Imperial Majesty into a very bad temper, and with good reason'.

Etienne Falconet was involved in the quarrel since it was he who was indirectly responsible for the situation which had arisen. Falconet was working on his famous equestrian statue of Peter the Great in St Petersburg from 1766–1768, at the time when the Empress had become dissatisfied with the heavy architectural style of her palaces; having heard of the new Neo-classicism so fashionable in the West, she was anxious to know more about it. In 1772, the year when Lvov's Russian edition of Palladio's *Quattro Libri* appeared, Falconet gave her a book of engravings of Roman ruins which appealed to her so much that the engraver, Cochin, was asked to nominate someone who could design 'a Graeco-Roman house' for her in her park at Tsarskoe Selo. The following year Cochin gave Clérisseau the nomination which had such dire results. A reconciliation was effected later but, fortunately for Cameron, Catherine's plans for new buildings were in abeyance for the next five years.

Another source of Cameron's introduction might have been Baron Melchior Grimm, a Bavarian, who came to St Petersburg for the first time in 1773 in order to attend the wedding of Catherine's son, the Grand Duke Paul, and the daughter of the Landgrave of Hesse-Darmstadt. Grimm had for some years been buying works of art for Catherine in Paris; now that they had actually met, their long correspondence continued in very friendly fashion. Grimm visited Russia again in 1776 and to the end of her life Catherine entrusted him with all her artistic commissions in France, and consulted him on any matters of note. But when she wrote to him about Cameron, as she did on 23 August 1779,

> Now I have secured *mister Cameron*, Scottish by nationality, Jacobite by persuasion, great designer trained in the antique manner, known for his book on the ancient Baths

this does not appear to be the type of letter that would have been written to the man who had recommended Cameron, and who would surely know all about him and his work. Reiffenstein, on the other hand and as we shall see later, had been instructed in April 1779 to look for two good Italian architects who would be willing to work for Catherine in St Petersburg, so he was definitely a man prospecting for new talent—for architects willing to work in Russia.

It might have been sufficient merely to send Cameron's book *The Baths of the Romans* to Her Imperial Majesty. The Empress was a great reader of books in several languages; she read widely in order to keep abreast of western thought, and when she considered that an author might be of use to her she summoned him to St Petersburg. This she had done, and with considerable courage, in 1768, when after reading Dr Thomas Dimsdale's *The Present Method of Inoculation for the Small-Pox* she invited him to her Court, and to encourage others had herself and her son successfully inoculated by him. So when she was looking for an architect who would work in the classical style—and construct baths for her—*The Baths of the Romans*[12] may have appeared almost as providential as had Dimsdale's book.

By whatever means Charles Cameron had been summoned to St Petersburg he did not hesitate to respond to the call when it came, and in the year 1779 he reached the city. He had sloughed off his old self and arrived with considerable panache—a romantic figure in his mid-thirties, a Scottish Jacobite of rank. Now, full of confidence, he was ready to take up his post as architect to the Empress of All the Russias, an honour which surely far exceeded the wildest dreams of the boy brought up in London, in Bolton Street and White Horse Street.

V

The Empress of All the Russias

When Charles Cameron first met Catherine the Great, she was a woman of fifty with very considerable charm, in whose face at this time the Prince de Ligne saw reflected 'genius and courage, calm and firmness'; according to all reports she carried herself superbly, giving a majestic impression of height which she did not in fact possess (Plate 8). She was every inch an Empress and very different from the little German princess who in 1744, at the age of fifteen, went to St Petersburg to be married to the Grand Duke Peter. Peter ascended the throne in 1761, on the death of his aunt, the Empress Elizabeth, but within a year he was dead, some said killed at the instigation of his wife, who on 28 June 1762 had been proclaimed Empress after a military coup d'état.

To establish herself on so precarious a throne was no easy task, but Catherine never faltered. There were many difficulties, but they were all surmounted. The most dangerous was a domestic revolt in 1773, led by a Cossack, Pugachev, who claimed that he, and not the man in the tomb in the Alexander Nevsky Monastery, was the Emperor Peter III; he advanced to within one hundred and twenty miles of Moscow before he was captured and executed. Also from 1766 onwards the war with Turkey, with all its perils, was always in the background, and it was not until the Russo-Turkish peace treaty of Kuchuk-Kainardji in 1774 that Catherine could relax her vigilance and seriously turn her mind to the embellishment of St Petersburg. As the spiritual heir of Peter the Great, for whom she had the highest veneration, she would inevitably have felt this to be her duty, but Catherine was a woman with the widest interests and there seems to be no reason to doubt her own statement that 'she made friends, liked work, loved society and delighted in the arts'.

It is probably true that she began her literary correspondence with such men as Voltaire and Diderot as a means of demonstrating to the rest of Europe that Russia was an emergent country with an enlightened and cultured ruler. No doubt it was also with the intention of opening a little wider Peter the Great's 'window on the west' so that Russia could learn more about the rest of Europe. Her letters were fully equal to the occasion; they reveal a powerful intellect and an acute political brain, as Bernard Pares said of her in his *History of Russia*:

39

Catherine was not merely a patron of the French encyclopaedists she was herself one of them and not by any means the least. Grimm tells us that after talking with her in her palace, he would walk in his room for hours before he could go to sleep. He describes her brilliance as like a fountain showering down in sparks.

Very early in her reign, advised by Diderot and her ambassador, Prince Galitzin, she began to buy pictures in Paris. Then she bought whole collections; the Crozat collection containing eight Rembrandts and Raphael's *Madonna and Child with St Joseph*, Count Brühl's collection from Dresden, which included four Rembrandts and five Rubens, and in 1779 she purchased for £36,000 Sir Robert Walpole's collection from Houghton Hall (198 pictures, including fifteen Van Dycks). At her death the imperial art collection contained nearly 4,000 pictures of remarkable quality. The collection was housed in the Hermitage, 'an edifice used by Catherine II both as a museum and a place of refuge from her court duties', which soon had to be enlarged.

By means of her correspondence and her official contacts in all the capitals of Europe, the Empress kept herself abreast of western thought. She had learnt from Falconet about the Neo-classical trend in western architecture, and in November 1778 she asked Reiffenstein to purchase for her a large number of Pannini's pictures of the interiors of Roman basilicas. Since Frederick the Great was one of her correspondents she must also have been well aware that two copies of Palladio's palazzos had been built in Potsdam in the 1750s; but she had to bide her time. Yet in July 1772 she had already begun to construct gardens in the English style, and wrote in a letter to Voltaire:

Now I love to distraction gardens in the English style, the curving lines, the gentle slopes, ponds like lakes, archipelagos on dry land, and I hold in contempt straight lines and twin alleys. I hate fountains which torture the water and force it into a course contrary to its nature, statues are consigned to the galleries, halls, etc. In a word anglomania rules my plantomania.[1]

All this reflects the influence of Lancelot Brown the English consulting gardener, trained under William Kent, who had first transformed the parks of English country gentlemen by abandoning stiff geometric patterns in favour of a natural landscape, knowing that this would be a perfect setting for their Palladian villas. In reality Brown (called 'Capability' because he always considered the 'capabilities' of the site to be laid out) was very subtly taming Nature; he developed expansive lawns and planted clumps of trees at strategic points and on the boundaries of parks, and always, if possible, he placed an artificial river or a serpentine lake somewhere in the middle distance. Brown's was the art which conceals art, for the simplicity of his effects was not obtained without artifice.

Since the Empress had never seen one of these new English gardens she could only visualise them from engravings and reading, and had the greatest difficulty in making her architect and gardener understand what she wanted. First of all she ordered them to leave the trees unclipped, then she told them that they should endeavour to follow nature. They did their best but, reports Mr Loudon (a pupil of Brown's who visited Russia in 1813), always without success:

> She did not know how to direct them exactly, yet she felt convinced that what they had done was not right, so she determined to get a landscape gardener from England to lay out her garden.[2]

This was about the year 1762; it took time to find the right person but at last John Busch (or Bush) of Hackney, the man who later became the father-in-law of Charles Cameron, was chosen for the post, preference being given to him because he could speak German. He appears to have been a most estimable character, and his landlord, Jeremiah Bentham (father of Jeremy) held him in high regard. In 1771 Busch 'gave up his establishment at Hackney with the nursery and foreign correspondence to Messrs Loddiges' and set off with his family for Russia.

The garden that Catherine wished him to lay out for her was at her palace of Tsarskoe Selo, set amidst a birch forest some fifteen miles from St Petersburg. This garden, about four miles in circumference, was still the original 'Dutch' garden with 'fish-canals, avenues, neat bowers, alleys, espaliers and close boskets with mossy seats'. It was this that Catherine wanted Busch to alter; but, first of all, she tested him by setting him to work on the hill of Pulkovo, half-way between Tsarskoe Selo and St Petersburg. Later on she visited him there:

> On entering the garden, and seeing a winding shady gravel walk planted on both sides, she appeared struck with surprise, and exclaimed 'This is what I wanted!' This walk led to a fine lawn, with gravel walks round it, which seemed to strike her still more forcibly and she again said, 'This is what I have long wished to have!' The following year the Tsarskoe Selo gardens were given to the charge of John Busch, who carried on the improvements till 1789 when he left the service of the Empress and returned to England.[3]

John Busch, with his wife and four daughters and his son Joseph, who succeeded him as the imperial head gardener, lived in a flat above the orangery at Tsarskoe Selo. Busch found Charles Cameron congenial, and must have given him a warm welcome on his arrival, for soon he provided him with a work-room in the flat. An unpublished diary in the possession of Sir John Dimsdale gives an interesting description of the life of the Busch family at this time. The diarist was Elizabeth Dimsdale, daughter of that Dr Dimsdale who had inoculated the Empress Catherine against smallpox in 1768. Elizabeth was visiting St Petersburg with her father in 1781 and in her diary for that year she recorded that she had dined with the Buschs: 'Had a good English dinner. Mrs Bush and four daughters agreeable people'. She mentioned other facts: 'Bush was paid a yearly salary of 19,000 roubles;

he had several hundred citrus trees to care for; he produced excellent fruit, and Mrs Bush fattened her turkeys on dried ants' eggs'.[4] Interesting information, but how much more interesting would have been a description of Charles Cameron in these new surroundings! Presumably, as Cameron was not present, he had not yet become engaged to Catherine Busch, whom he later married; the actual date of the wedding is unknown, but it was sometime between 1781 and 1784.

Tsarskoe Selo, the country seat of the Czars, had a romantic origin. In English the Russian words Tsarskoe Selo mean 'imperial village', but this very suitable name evolved from a very different original which was Sarskoié Sélo, the village of Saari, a Finnish word meaning 'high place'. So it was officially recognised until about 1725, and the village does indeed stand on a little plateau, making it a more salubrious spot than St Petersburg. This inspired a happy thought in the mind of Peter the Great's wife, Catherine; she contrived a surprise for her husband and, buying land near the village, secretly erected on it a stone villa, with a terrace and gardens in the Dutch style:

> When Peter returned from Poland, Catherine took him out to see a place calculated for the erection of a country residence. The Tsar was enchanted: 'the place to which my Catherine is taking us must indeed be charming, since the way to it is so beautiful'. The new edifice suddenly burst on His Majesty. Catherine: 'this is the villa which I have constructed for my sovereign'.
>
> The Tsar, in ecstasy, embraced his consort—on leaving the villa at night he was heard to say that he had passed one of the happiest days of his life.[5]

When Peter the Great's daughter, the Empress Elizabeth, came to the throne in 1741 she wished to retain Tsarskoe Selo but not the stone villa as a royal residence. She thought rather in terms of Versailles and employed the Italian architect, Rastrelli, to build a worthy palace for her. This he certainly did, as the three-storey façade of the palace he designed for her, nearly 1,200 ft in length, is said to be the longest in the world, and everything about it was on a similar stupendous scale. Elizabeth was delighted, and named it the Catherine Palace, in honour of her mother, Catherine I. The palace was then even more sumptuous than it is now, since, to conform with her taste, all the ornaments, pillars and caryatids were gilded 'with leaf-gold on oil . . . the value in gold amounted to above a million of ducats', and there was also a gilt balustrade running along the roof adorned with gilt vases and statues. The opulent effect desired by Elizabeth had been achieved; the villagers believed that the roof itself was made of solid gold! When the palace came into Catherine the Great's hands this decoration had weathered very badly and she had it repaired and stripped, the caryatids and so on all being covered in less gaudy paint. Dr Granville, an English traveller, has a story about these repairs which illustrates the Empress Catherine's lofty indifference to money:

Some of the contractors offered Her Majesty nearly half-a-million of roubles (silver) to be permitted to collect the fragments of gold which the weather had spared, but the Empress scornfully refused, saying, 'I am not in the habit of selling my old clothes!'

The observant Dr Granville remarked of the façade of the palace: 'Internally the whole of this stupendous line forms but one uninterrupted suite of apartments, the projecting portions of the front serving only to give more capacity to some of the rooms'. In other words, life in these state rooms, indeed in all this magnificent palace, was meant to be lived in public, in ostentation and luxury (Plate 12). This was all very well for the Empress Elizabeth, but it did not suit the Empress Catherine, who as early as 1764 had the Hermitage built so that she might enjoy privacy and relaxation in pleasant surroundings. Yet from the beginning of her reign she moved her court every summer from St Petersburg to Tsarskoe Selo.

It is not then surprising that as soon as possible after 1774, when the Turkish peace treaty permitted her to turn her mind from war to peace, she decided to modernise the palace. On 13 April 1778 she wrote to Grimm:

There is going to be a terrible upheaval in the domestic arrangements at Tsarskoe Selo. The Empress does not intend to live any longer in two unsuitable rooms; she is going to pull down the one and only staircase at the end of the house; she wants to live in the midst of the three gardens; she wants to have the same view from her windows as from the main balcony. The grand staircase has been moved to the small wing beside the entrance on the Gatchina side. She will have ten rooms and will ransack all the books in her library for designs for their decoration, and her imagination will have free rein—and everything will be like these two pages, that is to say devoid of common sense.

This letter rouses speculation. The last sentence suggests that Catherine's schemes had gone awry, as indeed they may have done if she had allowed the whole of Rastrelli's main staircase to be moved without proper architectural supervision. Perhaps this was the cause of the appeal she made to Grimm the following year, on 16 April 1779, begging him to ask Reiffenstein in Rome to send her two Italian architects:

He will have the kindness to write to the sublime Reiffenstein telling him to find two good architects, Italians and clever at their work, whom he will engage for the service of Her Imperial Majesty of All the Russias by a contract for a number of years, and he will despatch them from Rome to Petersburg like a bag of tools. He will not give them millions, but an honest and sensible salary, and he must choose honest and sensible men, not men like Falconet, their feet must be on the ground, not in the clouds. They should be directed to me, or to Baron Friedrichs, or to Count Bruce, or to M.d'Eck, or to M. Bexborodko, or to the devil and his grandmother—no matter, so long as they come, for all my architects have become too old, or too blind, or too slow, or too lazy, or too young, or too idle, or too grand, or too rich, or too set in their ways, or too scatter-brained . . . in a word, anything you like but not what I require.

Four months later, on 23 August 1779, she wrote the letter to Grimm telling him that she was now employing 'mister Cameron'. This is the first mention of Cameron's arrival, and the reason why his biographers have put the date as 1779. The hard fact is that no one has succeeded in tracing Cameron's movements from the time the 'Cameron Case' ended in London, culminating in Walter Cameron's committal to the Fleet on 29 August 1776, until the Empress Catherine comments on his work for her in 1779; so, until new evidence can be found, for all intents and purposes the date of Catherine's letter to Grimm on 23 August 1779 must be taken as the beginning of Cameron's working life in Russia. After telling Grimm how she had 'secured mister Cameron' she continued:

we are designing with him here a terraced garden, with baths below and gallery above; it will be something fine, fine,—to quote Maître Blaise.

VI

Tsarskoe Selo - The Catherine Palace

It was natural that the author of a book on *The Baths of the Romans* should immediately be asked to design a terraced garden with a gallery on top and baths below. As the editor of Loukomski's *Charles Cameron* points out:

> Baths had for centuries been a tradition and a habit in Russia. In old Muscovy it was not unusual for ministers to meet in the baths and discuss matters of State, thus combining work with healthy recreation . . . When Versailles was being built, of brick and stone in all its magnificence, it had not conveniences, let alone baths, yet at the same time Alexis, the second Romanov, invited Italian builders to construct a country house of wood (Kolomenskoe) which contained not only baths for the members of the family, but also three for the servants.

But, in fact, Cameron's baths, housed in the Agate Pavilion and completed only in 1785, were among the last buildings to be erected by him at Tsarskoe Selo.

The Empress must have considered that her own private apartments should first of all be made ready for her. If she were still living in the two 'unsuitable' rooms of which she had complained so bitterly to Grimm in April 1778 she must have been longing for something more comfortable, and Cameron was the very man to do the work for her. He could not have forgotten that one of the maxims in Isaac Ware's *Complete Body of Architecture* was that:

> The art of building cannot be more grand than it is useful; nor its dignity a greater praise than its convenience.

It seems most likely that in August 1779, so early in Cameron's career at the imperial court, he was fashioning with the Empress the scheme for his future work at Tsarskoe Selo. Confirmation of this appears in another letter written by Catherine to Grimm in the following May (16 May 1780), using the future tense:

> If you could see what a beautiful gallery and what beautiful terraced gardens I shall have beside my new suite of rooms at Tsarskoe Selo you would say that Kameron is a capable man; this Kameron is a near relative of Jennis Kameron, known for her devotion to the last of the Stuarts.

Ever since she wrecked Rastrelli's staircase Catherine must have decided that it was in that corner of the palace, the south-west, that she wished to place her new apartments, and indeed it was the only corner where Neo-classical additions could also be made without materially affecting the old Baroque building. New rooms were to spring up on the site of the staircase, in fact the whole right wing of the palace would be transformed by Cameron into something no less rich and rare, but much more intimate and restful. So far the changes were more decorative than constructional, but the plans had to be precise for the bath building which was to lie on the slope of a hill and would have to be connected with Catherine's new apartments. Cameron overcame this difficulty by linking up the two with a terrace on a rusticated base, the whole scheme ending with the famous Gallery or Colonnade, built on the site of a tennis court, which pleased Catherine so much that she gave it the name of the architect—a unique honour—and to this day it remains the Cameron Gallery, the KAMERONOVA GALLEREIA.

In 1779, however, that lay six years ahead, and Catherine, being a practical woman, decided that, just as she had tested her gardener, Busch, by first putting him to work at Pulkovo, so now she would test her architect Cameron by making him decorate a series of rooms at the other end of the palace before starting on her own. This, the 'First Apartment', is now known as the suite of the Empress Elizabeth Alexeievna, consort of Catherine's grandson, the Czar Alexander I, who resided there from 1815–25. This whole wing was destroyed by bombs during the Second World War but today it stands precisely as it did in Cameron's time, an incredibly successful piece of restoration meticulously carried out by Soviet architects and artists working from Cameron's own plans. It is composed of eight rooms: the Blue Drawing Room, Chinese Cabinet, Ante-Room, Green Dining Room, Bedroom, Music Room and two service rooms, and is simpler in style than Cameron's later work, because, being on trial, he had to use the materials that were available. Some, such as hardwoods for the flooring and marble for the fireplaces, were easily procurable, and Russian craftsmen had no difficulty in carrying out his designs for inlaid doors and parquet floors; for the latter the abundance and variety of Russian woods made possible intricate and beautiful designs in different colours (Plates 9 to 11).

The Empress was enraptured when she saw some of the finished rooms. She wrote to Grimm on 22 June 1781:

Clérisseau's work will be welcome. I have an architect here named Kameron, born a Jacobite, brought up in Rome. He is known for his book on the ancient Roman baths; the man has a fertile brain, and a great admiration for Clérisseau; so the latter's drawings will help Kameron to decorate my new apartments here, and these apartments will be superlatively good. So far only two rooms have been finished, and people rush to see them because they have never before seen anything like them. I admit that I have not grown tired of looking at them for the last nine weeks; they are pleasing to the eye.

46

No wonder Catherine and her court rushed to see these rooms, since in so short a time Cameron had made a complete break with established Russian architectural practice. It is difficult for the British, brought up now for two centuries in the classical Adam tradition of interior decoration, to appreciate just how great were Cameron's innovations in eighteenth-century St Petersburg. Gone were the heavy gilded limewood carvings above the doors, so beloved of Rastrelli, to be replaced by medallions and friezes with mythological designs; gone were the heavily carved chimney-pieces, giving place to the lighter and more delicate marble ones, and the range of colours, too, were different and much softer:

> The brilliant blues and golds, the strong clear hues which had characterised Tsarskoe Selo at the time of Elizabeth went out of fashion. Primaries were replaced by complementaries or by muted tones, bronze for gold, lavender for blue, olive and pistachio for bright green, and grey-blue for Elizabeth's favourite azure.[1]

The rooms were restful, small and comfortable. Catherine II had at last got what she wanted. So pleased was she that before the first rooms were finished she bade her Scottish architect start work on the south-west corner of the palace, and very soon the gap left by the removal of Rastrelli's staircase was filled by a more modest stair, a Rotunda and a Chinese Hall.

At this time Cameron also designed the church of St Sophia, for the village of Sophia which lay just outside the palace gates. The foundation stone must have been laid in 1782 because in the church there is, or was, a silver gilt trowel bearing the inscription 'Catherine II—Charles Cameron, architect 1782'. It is said that Cameron's first design for this church was unacceptable, and, if this is true, it was to be his one failure, which gives him an amazing record of success, especially as only three years previously, when he was summoned to Russia, he still apparently had not a single building to his credit. He must have possessed a great capacity for sheer hard work—latent though it seemed during his youth in England—and it was as well that this was so, because his arrival in Russia, fortuitously timed, coincided most fortunately with what the Empress Catherine herself described as her 'mania for building'. She wrote to Grimm on 23 August 1779:

> You should know that our mania for building is stronger than ever, and no earthquake can have destroyed more buildings than we are erecting. The mania for building is a diabolical thing; it consumes money, and the more one builds the more one wants to build; it is a disease like drunkenness.

Reiffenstein in Rome had succeeded in finding for her the two Italian architects she wanted. The famous Giacoma Quarenghi and the mediocre Trombara soon followed Cameron to St Petersburg. By 1783 Quarenghi was at work on the Academy of Sciences at St Petersburg and on a further addition to Catherine's extension of the Winter Palace, the Hermitage

Theatre, and other buildings. By 1783 Cameron had completed the 'First Apartment' in the Catherine Palace and was half-way through his decoration of the private suite, the 'Fifth Apartment', which the Empress occupied the following year.

The Empress Catherine was always supremely happy during her summer sojourn at Tsarskoe Selo; she would arrive in April or May and enjoy the informal life she was able to lead there. She worked just as hard, keeping her Winter Palace routine of early rising and dealing with official business during the morning and early afternoon; after that she cast ceremony aside. She would go out, wearing a plain dress, to mingle with her subjects in the park, which was always open to the public, or to exercise her favourite greyhound, 'Sir Tom Anderson', and his numerous progeny. When she had guests she invited them to join her at a simple supper, followed by cards or conversation—rarely music, for which she had no ear.

When diplomats came from St Petersburg she received them in her new official suite, the 'Fourth Apartment': perhaps in the Arabesque Room (Plate 27), the Lyons Drawing Room, or in the Silver Room where she dealt with much official correspondence. She was enchanted by all the new rooms, and even more by those in her own private suite. It is unfortunate that today no visitors can see them, nor will they be able to do so until war damage repairs have been completed. Descriptions of them can be obtained only from those who saw them before 1941 and from old photographs in Loukomski, but all these confirm Catherine's prescience when, in 1781, she wrote to Grimm that 'these rooms will be superlatively good'.

Part of Cameron's success may have been due to the manner in which each room was so admirably suited to its purpose. The reception rooms comprising the 'Fourth Apartment' could not have been less like the adjacent Great Hall which Rastrelli, inspired by the Galerie des Glaces at Versailles, had built for the Empress Elizabeth. Yet Cameron's smaller Arabesque Room, Lyons Drawing Room and Chinese Hall, with their perfection of proportion, decoration and design, made an equally splendid, if more intimate setting for the Empress Catherine when she was engaged in her official duties.

In the 'Fifth Apartment', containing the Empress's private rooms, Cameron would appear to have been at his most imaginative. Through three centuries visitors have commented on the charm of these 'miniature rooms', so small yet so complete, so delicately decorated in 'opalescent milky white, blue and green'. The tiny Blue Room with its blue glass columns and festoons of tinted bronze, gained the name of the 'Tabatière', because of a fancied resemblance to the richly decorated and enamelled snuff-boxes of the period.

Beside the 'Tabatière' was the Empress's bedroom, and on this bedroom Cameron lavished all his skill. It was light and bright, and very feminine;

9 The Blue Drawing Room in the First Apartment in the Catherine Palace, Tsarskoe Selo.

10 Free-standing porcelain pillars in the Bedroom in the First
Apartment of the Catherine Palace, Tsarskoe Selo.

11   Stuccowork in the Green Dining Room in the First
Apartment of the Catherine Palace, Tsarskoe Selo.

Дворецъ Ея Императорскаго Величества въ Сарскомъ Селѣ
въ 25 ти Верстахъ отъ Санктпетербурга.

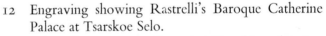
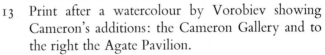

Maison de Plaisance de Sa Maj.^{té} Imp.^{le} de toutes les Russies &c. &c. &c.
à Sarskoe Selo, 25 Verstes de St Petersbourg

12 Engraving showing Rastrelli's Baroque Catherine Palace at Tsarskoe Selo.

13 Print after a watercolour by Vorobiev showing Cameron's additions: the Cameron Gallery and to the right the Agate Pavilion.

14 The Agate Pavilion at terrace and ground level, showing
its site between Rastrelli's palace and Cameron's Gallery.

15　The rusticated ramp with its Renaissance-style masks and the Cameron Gallery with the bronze busts of Catherine's heroes.

The entrance of the Gymnase of the pre-revolutionary time?

the main colour scheme was lilac, and the slender moulded glass columns here reappeared in a shade of deep violet with small bases and capitals of bronze; between the columns were mirrors, and the walls were covered with milky glass decorated with bronze eagles and sphinxes. The ceiling was of glass, overlaid with bronze, and its circular motif was repeated in reversed form in the floor, in various coloured woods; from the ceiling hung a tremendous three-tier chandelier in gilded bronze and rock crystal, and the lamps on the walls were also of rock crystal. The marble over-mantel was decorated in white amethyst and gold, and, like the mantelpiece, it was studded with Wedgwood medallions, imported from England (Plate 30).

It is obvious that no expense had been spared, but Catherine was content, and Cameron must have fully appreciated the magnitude of his good fortune in having secured such a rich and influential patron. Catherine the Great had behind her the wealth and power of 'all the Russias'; she was an autocrat answerable only to herself, she could give Cameron commission after commission; moreover, she trusted him sufficiently to allow him to work in his own way, with no interference from her once her requirements were understood. She was indeed the patron of whom every artist dreams, but few encounter.

VII

The Agate Pavilion
and Cameron Gallery

Until the private apartments were completed Cameron had been working on interior decoration only, on improvements to another man's palace, Rastrelli's. Now he had to build his own additions to that palace, the Agate Pavilion and the Cameron Gallery, and to build them in Neo-classical style, to suit the Empress's taste for this more severe contemporary form of architecture. In the flood of her enthusiasm he was also commissioned to design the palace of Pavlovsk for her son. He soon discovered that interior decorating in Russia and the actual construction of new buildings posed very different problems.

The Russians had a long tradition of building in wood, but not in stone, and when, in 1784, Cameron began the construction of the Agate Pavilion his troubles were not far to seek. His Russian biographer, Taleporovski, describes them in some detail. In the first place Cameron had some difficulty in making the Russian contractors understand what he wanted; he also discovered that, when his back was turned, lead could be spirited away, and inferior timber and stone substituted for the good quality materials he had specified. He complained of the contractors' dishonesty; the contractors retaliated by complaining that he drew up his plans vaguely, and they could not understand them. Then curious 'calamities' occurred: nails, for instance, were hammered in so hard by the joiners that they penetrated decorated panels and even pierced water pipes, stupidity which must surely have seemed premeditated. Such a state of things could not be allowed to continue, and it was inevitable that in 1784 Cameron's thoughts should despairingly turn to his fellow countrymen and that he should make an effort to induce them to come over to work for him.

On 21 January 1784 the following advertisement appeared in the *Edinburgh Evening Courant:*[1]

> For her Majesty the Empress of all the Russias
> Wanted
> Two clerks, who have been employed by an Architect or very considerable Builder, who can draw well, such as figures and ornaments for rooms, etc, etc.
> Two Master Masons

Two Master Bricklayers
A Master Smith who can make locks, hinges, etc
Several Journeymen Plasterers
Several Journeymen Bricklayers
It is repeated that none will apply who are not fully masters of the above work, and who cannot bring with them proper certificates of their abilities and good behaviour. The master masons, bricklayers and smith must have been employed as Foremen in their different lines. The master bricklayers and men will have a pice (sic) of Ground given them. As the encouragement to each will be considerable, the best of tradesmen will be expected. For further particulars apply to Messrs Peter and Francis Forrester and Company, Leith, who will have a good vessel ready to carry them out by the 1st April next provided the Baltic is by that time open.

The choice of this newspaper was perhaps not surprising. Cameron, Jacobite by inclination as well as reputation, had to take his Scottish heritage very seriously, and it is possible he remembered that his grandfather was 'Archibald Cameron of Edinburgh' and that he might still have had relatives in that city. On the more practical side there was a considerable amount of trade between Leith and St Petersburg, and the firm of Messrs Peter & Francis Forrester & Co, providing transport to Russia, was a well established and reputable one. Was it not possible that the two clerks, for drawing 'figures and ornaments for rooms, etc' who had to produce proof of employment 'by an Architect or very considerable Builder', might, with any luck, turn out to be trainees of Robert Adam? Unfortunately there is no list in existence giving the names of the men who answered the advertisement, though a very large number did. The advertisement, it should be noted, concentrated on Master Masons, Master Bricklayers, Journeymen Plasterers and Bricklayers, all the trades required for actual building work, and the fact that the Master Masons and Bricklayers had to be trained Foremen showed that Cameron intended in future to have his own men in authority.

On 3 May 1784, the selected craftsmen, sixty or seventy of them, many of them with their wives and children, sailed from Leith for Kronstadt in the brig 'Betsey and Brothers'. Among the Seafield Papers in H.M. Register House, Edinburgh, there is a letter which two young men, William and George Lyon, sailing with their father, wrote to their mother telling her of their safe arrival in Russia:

(Tsarskoe Selo)

Zaskazelle
6 July 1784

Dear Mother,
    We are realy sencible of our long silence and likewise the uneasiness of mind which will rest on you till this come to your relief which most not be imputed to us as being neglectful, as no opertunities worth the trusting favoured us.

We are obliged to wait the return of the ship which is much longer than we expected as we landed on May 23. The ship has layng here ever since the above deat. Dear mother, we should thank God that we had so fine a passage and keeps our healths so well and free of all accidents. We had the finest weather and the quickest passage that has been sailed this long time. Very few passengers in the ship escaped sickness but ourselves, my father especially who was re-marked to be the only man among the passengers who stood the fatigue best. We was only about 12 days on sea. We halted at Elsinore, a place belonging to the king of Denmark where all ships bound for the Baltick most pay tribute or the fort will fire on all atempting to escape, and from that place passingers gets each a passport which serves them throw all Russia as you cannot go above 5 miles without showing your pass. Elsinore being half way we weighed from that throw the Straits and the same afternoon we sailed past Copmehagen the capital of Denmark where the king stays. We had a pleasant vue of Sweden on the one side and Denmark on the other side. Our first landing in Russia was at Cronstade, a place where ships from all nations of the glob comes to tread (trade), and when you come in vue of this place you would take it to be a very large wood. The ships all ly along side of one another and are lined out in streets for to let small ships or boats pass throw. In this place we staid 3 days, and Mr Cameron was sent for to Pettersburg which is 15 miles from Cronstead. He cam on all heast (haste) himself and his wife, accompanied by Mr Forester. The(y) were very glad to see us and gave us a grand treat at a teavron (tavern). From hence we set out for Pettersburg in a small ship, where we landed in 2 hours at the English taveron: there is but one in the town. Here we was ordered to stay till places or houses would be provided for us. So we have been a fortnight in this taveron where we was ordred to want for nothing but call for what ever we wanted. This orders came from the Empress. We hade tea for b(r)eakfast, all kinds of flesh, both rost and boild, for denner, and plainty of English strong ale, the same for supar. Here we had nothing to do but stroll about and vue the curiosities of the town, which is 6 miles square, 24 miles in circomference. This town is very regular built, with kinals in every street. The Empress has 2 grand palaces in the town, one of which is marrable (marble), and a new marrable church which is building just now. I shall endeavour to give you more larger and better descriptions of the place and maners of the people in my next which will be in a month after this before another letter can be sent, at least before it arrives in Edinburgh, as I mean to write by post. There is no possibily (possibility) of getting any money raised at present as the Empress only pais 4 times in the year. Than (Then) she pais in great sooms (sums). It is out of Mr Cameron's own poket that we are subsisted till the end of the quarter. The Empress is pleased just now to give us a chance of a prize which will be drawn by lotry tikets. The prize is a hous which the Empress means throw curiosity to give away. This hous is valued about 4000 roubles. It will amount to upwards of 6£ apiece to each man. The tikets is to be drawn next week. We are 14 miles out of Pietersburgh at the Empress sumar palace which is called Zeska Zellae. All that 15 miles betwixt Petersburgh and the sumar palace is ful of lamps on both sides of the road and large marrable pillars at the end of every mile. This road is one straight line and as leavel as it can be without the least interruption of a height. We are stationed in this place as yet as the most of the work lies here. Dear mother, I expect we will do very well here and in a short time relive (relieve) you and our selvs. When you write you will direct to the care of Mr Francis Forester, St Petersburgh, but I will write you again befor you will need to send me an answer. I have not much more to say at present, but remember us to all friends, Mrs Grant in particular, Sir James' family, not forgetting Mrs and Mr Warren and all our relations. Remember me to Jean Cuming and Marain Cuming and all that inquears for us.

Dear mother, we are your afectionate sons and with our dear father

WILLIAM LYON

GEORGE LYON

P.S.

The weather is very hot here. Just now they have the pleasantest and the finst nurishing sumer that can be in this place. The country is remarkable leavel (level). There is not the least hill to be seen throughout all the country. We can see as far as our eye can carry on plain ground.

After some initial difficulties all went well. Cameron had houses built for the men in the village of Sophia, and an imperial *ukase* regulated their hours of work: until 6 p.m. in spring and summer, with an extension to 9 p.m. if necessary, with a break for dinner at 2 o'clock, and special arrangements for Sundays and holidays.[2] Some of the craftsmen extended their contracts till the work was finished, others settled down for life. Everybody was happy except Mr Alleyne Fitz Herbert, the British ambassador at St Petersburg, who was horrified by the extent of this loss of useful subjects. Soon after the arrival of the ship, on 8 June, he sent the following despatch to the Marquis of Carmarthen in London:

I am sorry to inform Your Lordship that there arrived lately on board some ships from Leith a considerable number of stone masons, bricklayers and other artificers of the same class all from Edinburgh and its neighbourhood, who have been sent for by Mr Cameron, a British architect in the service of the Empress, in order to complete some extensive building which he is now employed upon at Czarskoe-Zelae. Many have likewise brought their wives and families as I am assured of no fewer than 140 persons. They are mostly engaged twelve months and it is to be hoped that when this term shall be expired they will return to their country; however, I need not point out to Your Lordship the various ill consequences which must result even from the temporary loss of so many useful subjects nor how necessary it is to take every possible precaution in order to prevent such emigration in future. Indeed it seems somewhat extraordinary that the Magistracy of Edinburgh should not have exerted themselves so as to prevent the artificers I have just been speaking of from leaving the Kingdom as people of that class are evidently included, not only within the meaning, but within the exact letter of the various acts of Parliament which have passed of late years in order to prevent the emigration of our manufacturers and as their embarkation was carried on, not by stealth, but in the most public manner. In addition to which, they were also, as it seems, collected together by public advertisements.[3]

The reference to 'Mr Cameron' in the letters of the brothers Lyon is the only personal reminiscence of him from a British source, and it raises the question, what manner of man was he, this enigmatic Scottish architect with, admittedly, rather a dubious youthful record? The Lyons obviously found him charming and generous; he had come post haste to meet them, given them a 'grand treat' at a tavern and, until their first pay-day, paid their expenses out of his own pocket. These do not appear to be the actions of a dour or mean Scotsman. A Scotsman he unmistakably was; he neither spoke Russian, nor dressed as a Russian. It has been suggested that his ignorance of the language made his later 'colleagues and collaborators not very sympathetic',[4] but, as the language of the Court was French, most of his fellow architects would also have been able to converse in that tongue. As long as Cameron was working directly for the Empress she saw to it that everything went as smoothly as possible, but there were many quarrels and misunderstandings when he came to work for her son, the Grand Duke Paul. Loukomski, however, states, without giving any grounds for the statement:

> There was nothing in his character to indicate that he was otherwise than very modest and agreeable, and if lavish in the use of valuable materials and rather slow in producing accounts, yet scrupulously honest.

With a similar lack of references for his statements Christopher Marsden, author of *Palmyra of the North*, describes Cameron as:

> Not an easy character to deal with, prodigal and temperamental, the 'poet-architect' as he was called.

In the next phase of his development Cameron was in truth a 'poet-architect'. The very names of his decorative materials have a ring of poetry: jasper and agate, malachite and lapis-lazuli, alabaster and porphyry, these were the materials with which he constructed the Agate Pavilion, possibly his finest work. The Agate Pavilion, with the Baths below, was the peak to which all the arduous fieldwork in Rome, the drawing and measuring, the careful investigation of the Baths of Titus and Diocletian, the compilation of *The Baths of the Romans* had led (Plates 4 and 25). The façade consisted of two niched pavilions, linked by a semi-circular gallery of Ionic pillars. On the top floor were six rooms, including the famous Great Hall and Jasper Room, and a library; this floor gained its name of Agate Pavilion from Cameron's lavish use of this stone, some of the interior walls being 'made of small pieces of agate and malachite cunningly pieced together'.[5] In these rooms Cameron seemed to be reacting to his more recent Russian environment in his search for the exotic in colour and materials. Catherine II once boasted to Voltaire that marble quarried in her empire could equal any in Italy, and now all varieties were being brought to Cameron: red and black, green and grey and white, they came to him from Finland, Karelia and

Siberia; from Siberia also and from the Urals came the malachite, the agate and the porphyry. With great skill he used them together or in contrast to produce the rich and polychrome effects which Mr Harold Macmillan, another Scot, found 'barbarically splendid', when he visited Tsarskoe Selo in 1932, and which can still be seen today.

To the French Minister Plenipotentiary, the Comte de Ségur, whom Catherine escorted round her palace, these additions seemed a veritable fairyland:

> Catherine II was so very kind as to show me all the beauties of this magnificent country house where the clear waters, the fresh woodland, the elegant pavilions, the noble architecture, the valuable furniture, the rooms panelled in porphyry, in lapis-lazuli and in malachite, had an air of fairy-land, and the travellers admiring them were reminded of the palace and gardens of Armide.

As the Agate Pavilion approached completion Cameron could concentrate on his final work at the palace of Tsarskoe Selo, his famous covered gallery with the Ionic colonnade—the Cameron Gallery. It delighted Catherine because it incorporated everything that she had most wanted: external classical simplicity and charm clothing an eminently practical interior, a central glazed gallery where she could go when it rained, with doors opening on to the colonnade, where she could walk or sit when the weather was fine, the entrance being just beyond the Agate Pavilion (Plates 13, 14, 15), on the terrace which led from her own apartments. Between each of the Ionic columns, on the inside, stood a bronze bust of one of the 'philosophers of antiquity'. Thirty of Catherine's favourite philosophers were there and, strangely enough, among them, between Demosthenes and Cicero, stood the bust of a contemporary, an Englishman—Charles James Fox! 'By his eloquence', Catherine explained, he had prevented England from going to war with Russia; 'I have no other way of expressing my gratitude', and she added, 'Pitt will be jealous!' According to Sir James Harris, British Ambassador at St Petersburg, 'the Empress had an almost romantic admiration of Mr Fox'. But alas, in 1789 at the outbreak of the French Revolution, when she discovered that Mr Fox's views differed so entirely from her own, Mr Fox's bust was removed and consigned to the rubbish heap.

At the end of the Gallery doors lead out to an impressive open staircase which first divides into two curving branches descending to the lower floor entrance, where a further straight and wide flight of stone steps leads down to the garden (Plate 16). These steps are set between high walls at the end of which stand, one on either side, bronze statues of Hercules and Flora Farnese. The effect is original and pleasing. As Catherine grew older, the time came when she could no longer climb so steep a stair, and it was then that Cameron devised for her the Pente Douce, a gentle inclined ramp leading directly down to the garden from a point on the terrace almost opposite the Agate Pavilion (Plate 15).

In 1785 the 'Cameron Gallery' was finished and there was no more work left to be done at Tsarskoe Selo. When, in 1779, Catherine had written to Grimm so crossly about her architects, the term 'lazy' might well have been relative. Cameron had met her requirements—and punctually too—but to have done so he must have been stretched to the limit; for he was at the same time expected to design and supervise a palace for the Grand Duke Paul at Pavlovsk, which was already habitable in 1785, but far from finished. It is true that Cameron had an office at Tsarskoe Selo, where a large staff of highly skilled assistant draughtsmen of various nationalities was working for him; nevertheless his post at Court, something which his British contemporaries might envy, was certainly no sinecure.

VIII

Pavlovsk

Relations between Catherine II and her son, the Grand Duke Paul, were, to say the least, strained. This, however, is not the place to discuss his traumatic childhood and the suggestions that he was not the son of the Czar Peter III. When Cameron first met Paul in 1779 he was twenty-five years old, a widower who had remarried, and was in search of an architect. His first wife Nathalie, daughter of the Landgrave of Hesse-Darmstadt, (at whose wedding in 1773 the Empress had made the acquaintance of her Paris correspondent, Baron Melchior Grimm) died in April 1776 after giving birth to a still-born child. A few months later his mother chose another bride for him, the seventeen-year-old Princess Sophia-Augusta of Würtemberg, and the marriage took place before the end of the year, when the princess received the Russian style and title of Grand Duchess Marie Feodorovna. In December 1777 their first child, the future Alexander I, was born, and a second son, Constantine, in 1779, followed by two more sons and six daughters.

Paul may or may not have been the son of Peter III, but he was devoted to his memory and had the same love for Prussia, the same love of military display—though not of war. He disagreed with his mother over her foreign policy and over much else, and she allowed him no share in her government, a fact which he deeply resented. In the Grand Duchess Marie he found an ally who supported him, and was prepared to take his side against her mother-in-law. She was a serious-minded young woman whom Catherine found dull, but she appears to have been genuinely fond of her rather tiresome, and latterly very difficult husband. The birth of their son Alexander in 1777, making the dynasty secure, produced a temporary softening of hearts; Catherine wept for joy at her grandson's baptism and gave his parents the estate which later was to be known as Pavlovsk. It is a few miles south of Tsarskoe Selo, charmingly situated beside the river Slavianka, among birch and pine forests. Paul and his wife were delighted with it and built two rustic chalets there, which they called Paullust and Marienthal; only when three years had passed, in 1780, did they decide to erect a permanent building in stone, to be called Pavlovsk in the Grand Duke's honour.

Cameron had already been asked to design a Temple of Friendship (an optimistic symbol, some say, of friendship between Catherine and her son) and by 1780 it was standing in the grounds with its famous Doric columns, sixteen of them, supporting a low dome and forming a circle round a statue of Catherine II, portrayed as Ceres, 'the benefactress'. The Empress admired the building, which she thought very beautiful (Plate 18) but declared that the interior was too dark, a fault which, fortunately, Cameron was able to remedy.[1]

It was not until the following year that a firm decision was taken to build a new palace and to give Cameron the post of architect. At last his chance had come to construct something in a truly Palladian style, and this he did (Plate 19); he produced a building standing on a bank of the river Slavianka which exactly suits its setting, and bears the stamp of his genius.

The palace of Pavlovsk is very attractive from any angle, and though for a palace it is surprisingly small this commission in fact took a very long time to complete. Cameron was to find in the Grand Duchess a far more exacting patron than the Empress. As it turned out, Marie-Feodorovna took a very great interest in the whole project, but instead of leaving Cameron alone as Catherine had done, she interfered at every point, criticising and trying to change his half-finished plans, and writing angry letters to him when she was abroad. The archives of Pavlovsk were full of acrimonious correspondence.[2] A good example of one of the 'misunderstandings' that continually occurred[3] is when the royal couple travelling incognito, thinly disguised as the Count and Countess of the North, made a grand tour of Europe which lasted from September 1781 to November 1782. They visited Vienna, Paris, Florence and Rome, and when they were in Rome Cameron wrote to the Grand Duchess asking if it would be possible for her to arrange for casts from the Villa Medici to be sent to him, as he would like to make use of them in his own work. The Grand Duchess acceded to this request and the casts were sent to him, but they were so badly damaged by damp in transit that they were useless when they arrived at St Petersburg; finally a day of reckoning came when Cameron himself was held responsible for their loss!

In Paris the Count and Countess of the North were received at the Court of Louis XVI, and Madame Campan, in her *Memoirs of Marie-Antoinette*, gives a description of their reception which reveals that Cameron was not alone in finding the Grand Duchess Marie-Feodorovna difficult:

The plain unassuming appearance of Paul pleased Louis XVI . . . The countess du Nord was not at first so successful with the Queen. This lady was of a fine height, very fat for her age, with all the stiffness of the German demeanour, well informed, and, perhaps, displayed her acquirements with rather too much confidence. At the moment the count and countess du Nord were presented, the Queen was exceedingly intimidated. She withdrew into her closet before she went into the room where she was to dine with the illustrious travellers, and asked for a glass of water, confessing, 'she had just experienced how much more difficult it was to play the part of a Queen in the presence of other sovereigns, or of princes born to become so, than before courtiers'.

She soon recovered from her first confusion, and made her reappearance with ease and confidence. The dinner was tolerably cheerful, and the conversation very animated.

The Grand Duke and his Duchess were much impressed by all they saw in France. Louis XVI gave the Grand Duke six Savonnerie carpets as a parting gift, and Marie-Antoinette gave his wife a magnificent Sèvres porcelain toilet set decorated with enamel on gold. Paul and Marie were entirely won over by the fragile 'Louis XVI' style; they bought pictures in Paris, and furniture from the best ébénistes—and then they came home to find a Neo-classical palace, and their chief reception room decorated after the manner of Robert Adam.

It may be that Catherine and Cameron, during those fourteen months when they worked together over the plans for the new palace during the absence of its future owners, were thinking too much in terms of their own taste and not making sufficient allowance for the modern outlook of the younger generation.

The Grecian Hall at Pavlovsk has often been compared with Adam's Great Hall at Kedleston, and it looks as though Cameron consciously based his design on that of Adam, possibly at the suggestion of the Empress. Towards the end of her life, in 1794, she wrote to Grimm 'I have all the works of the Adam brothers', and this must refer to the *Works in Architecture of Robert and James Adam*, published in three parts, in 1773, 1779, and 1822; the first two parts Catherine very likely bought on publication, and by 1782 could easily have digested them. Although they contain detailed prints and plans of Syon House, Kenwood and Luton Hoo, Kedleston does not figure on their pages, but Adam's plans for it can be found in Woolfe & Gandon's continuation of *Vitruvius Britannicus*, Vol. IV (1767) a copy of which must have been on the shelves of Cameron's extensive library, as probably would have been Paine's *Noblemen's and Gentlemen's Houses*, with his original plans for Kedleston.

The Grecian Hall at Pavlovsk was badly damaged during the last war, but has now been fully restored (Plate 21). Two authorities, at least, consider it to be Cameron's best work: Louis Réau called it 'Cameron's masterpiece', and George Heard Hamilton considers that the 'spacious Grecian Hall is Cameron's most successful palatial interior'. The critics have not thought as highly of the adjacent Italian Hall but in its different way—and Cameron here was drawing on his memories of Rome and of the Imperial Baths— it produces its desired effect (Plate 20).

Definitely these halls were works of art not to be confused with the 'Louis XVI' style and, whatever it cost him, Cameron did well to stand firm in his resistance to Marie-Feodorovna's meddling. The Empress Catherine had understood the architect's conception of the whole, the idea that Robert Adam also imposed upon his patrons; that everything in a room, down to the door-knobs and fire-dogs, must harmonise and be designed by the architect and by him alone. The Grand Duchess did not abide by these rules; it mattered little to her if the ceiling of her Dressing-Room had been inspired by ancient originals, she wished to display in it her new furniture from Paris and her priceless Sèvres. All through the years 1782–86 the quarrels went on, made all the worse because protocol demanded that communication between Cameron and the Grand Duchess had to be carried out through a third party, the 'Director' of the building operations at Pavlovsk.

The Director's name was Kuechelbecker, and he is described by Loukomski as 'a rather pedantic and tiresome German' who was much worried by Cameron's extravagance. Kuechelbecker was in an unenviable position, acting as a buffer between the Grand Duchess and Cameron, but he does not appear to have made the best of a bad job, nor to have been a very efficient Director. In September 1782, just before the return of the Grand Ducal couple from their Grand Tour, he had permitted the Russian carpenters at Pavlovsk to set up joists when Cameron was not there to supervise them, although this was contrary to the official instructions he had received. Naturally, when Cameron discovered what had happened he was angry, but he wrote a restrained letter to Kuechelbecker explaining that it was essential that he should be present on such occasion to see that sound material was used, and that the work was correctly executed; in this particular case he found that the joists had been wrongly placed, and the whole thing had to be done over again. He concluded with an assurance that he would see to it that the work at Pavlovsk was satisfactorily finished—both for the sake of his own reputation and for the honour of Scotland, his native country. Kuechelbecker was not impressed. He replied curtly that Cameron was being 'dilatory', and he must make every effort to speed up the building of Pavlovsk.[4]

Kuechelbecker was, of course, the Director at Pavlovsk; he cared nothing for Tsarskoe Selo and Cameron's labours there, and Cameron found himself in an extremely difficult position, made no easier when the Grand Duchess returned home and began her constant nagging. On one occasion she objected to the colour and design of Cameron's carefully chosen wall coverings. On another she spoke on behalf of her husband, and Kuechelbecker may not have been ill pleased to pass on the message: 'to beg Cameron, in God's name . . . to produce designs for decorations which accord with Pavel Petrovitch's taste!'

Loukomski suggested that this somewhat one-sided correspondence throws a certain amount of light on Cameron's character:

He was very sure of himself and accurate in his decisions. He was an independent artist whose conceptions were clear and simple, whose taste was classical and restrained. He would have been quicker to sacrifice his own ideas than to renounce the classical ideal. He considered that one copy of an ancient building was worth more than all modern creations.[5]

If Marie-Feodorovna saw Cameron in this light it is easy to understand how terribly old-fashioned she and her husband must have thought him, and in fact there was more to their quarrels than the placing of furniture and the colour of a curtain. She disliked the polychrome effects and the Pompeian arabesques and medallions that he had used with such effect at Tsarskoe Selo, and believed them to be not only in bad taste, but bad in terms of design; the medallions, she said, were 'monotonous'. The Grand Duke Paul was, of course, almost certain to dislike any design his mother had approved. Yet Loukomski assures us that Cameron made a good impression on the Grand Duchess at their first meeting, 'but he frightened her by his prodigality. He worked very rapidly as through the guidance of inspiration'.[6]

If this is true, it was indeed fortunate for Cameron, because from 1782–85 he needed to work fast to finish the Agate Pavilion and the Cameron Gallery. In regard to his 'prodigality' and 'extravagance' which so worried the Grand Duke, the Grand Duchess and Kuechelbecker, it cannot be denied that Cameron demanded the best of everything—gilt bronze, marble, fine wood, semi-precious stones, skilled craftsmanship. But it must have been difficult for him, working simultaneously at Tsarskoe Selo and Pavlovsk, to remember that what the Empress would willingly give him at one place, the Grand Duke would deny him at the other.

Meanwhile the outside world had not been standing still while Cameron built his fairy palaces. In 1786, he was summoned away from Pavlovsk to play his part in the preparations then being made by Potemkin for Her Imperial Majesty's triumphal tour of the Crimea in the following year.

IX

The Crimea

Gregory Alexandrovitch Potemkin was at the height of his power in 1786. He had been born at Smolensk in the Ukraine in 1739, the son of a retired army captain, and, entering the army himself and taking part, under Count Orlov, in the coup d'état which placed Catherine on the throne, he soon gained rapid promotion. He was ten years younger than the Empress and for two years, from 1774–76, he was her lover, but, unlike the others, when the affair became platonic he was not dismissed from Court: on the contrary, he remained to become her chief adviser as well as commander-in-chief of her armies. He was a strangely fascinating character, a patriot and a wayward genius: a man of moods, ostentatious, often indolent, but capable of immense effort when it was required of him, with a quick, original mind, and boundless ambition. He had a greater ascendancy over Catherine than any other person; she loaded him with gifts and honours, calling him 'bold mind, bold spirit, bold heart', and together they schemed and planned to extend the Russian borders to the south, extend them perhaps until they had created a new Byzantine empire. The first Turkish war had achieved much, but Catherine dreamed of more, of gaining access first to the Black Sea, then to the Mediterranean, and ultimately of driving the Turks from Constantinople.

Ever since the end of the first Turkish war in 1774 Russia had had difficulty with the Tartar chiefs in the Crimea, independent of Turkey in the terms of the peace treaty although the Sultan retained the right to appoint these khans, many of whom were still loyal to him. But at last one of them, the Khan Shagin of Crimea, was induced to place himself and his people under the protection of Russia, and promptly, on 8 April 1783, the Empress signed a manifesto proclaiming the annexation of the Crimea, explaining that her patience was exhausted by all the previous insurrections and revolts. The Turks could do little about it, and the following year, 1784, they signed the Treaty of Constantinople, accepting Russia's annexation, and granting her free passage through the Dardanelles and access to the Black Sea. In gratitude, the Empress appointed Potemkin President of the Council of War —with the rank of field-marshal—and made him governor-general of the Crimea and the other conquered provinces, for which the Taurida was the old geographical name. For his part Potemkin promised Catherine that he would turn the whole of the Crimea 'into one vast garden for her pleasure', but that was to prove a heavy task.

There was much to be done: the vast spaces had to be 'settled', made suitable for a manufacturing and agricultural rather than a nomadic people, towns and villages had to be constructed so that the Empress's new subjects might enjoy as she had promised, 'all the advantages enjoyed by her ancient subjects'. So it was not until 1786 that Potemkin saw his way clear to devise with her a tour of inspection of his work in the Crimea; that at least was the reason given for her journey, but it was much more than that; it was a royal progress intended to dazzle her allies and intimidate her enemies. The Empress was to leave St Petersburg on 14 January 1787 and travel via Smolensk to Kiev, where she would embark on a galley to take her down the Dnieper as far as the rapids (rocks in the way being blown up to level the river bed), then on by road to Cherson, at the mouth of the Dnieper, and thence to the Crimea to stay at Bakhtchisarai, the ancient capital of Tartarian Taurida, in the palace of the last khan of the Crimea. The return would be by road to Moscow, with a judicious stop on the way at Poltava (scene of Peter the Great's historic victory over the Swedes on 27 June 1709) and in July the Empress would be back again in St Petersburg.

The part allotted to Cameron in this grandiose scheme was that of restorer of the Khan's palace at Bakhtchisarai; his aim, to transform it into a suitable imperial residence, a commission for which Isaac Ware and Palladio had not prepared him. According to Potemkin's German biographer the palace was 'a compound of Moorish, Arabian, Chinese and Turkish architecture, with fountains, little gardens, paintings, gilt ornaments and inscriptions in every corner'.[1] Loukomski commends Cameron for having 'succeeded in preserving on the whole the fifteenth century style', and the Empress must have approved of his efforts since she commanded that it was 'to be kept in repair, and always according to its present Oriental form'. Whether Cameron was fully occupied by this work at Bakhtchisarai, or whether he was also engaged on some of the new buildings erected along the route for Catherine's overnight stops, there is no means of knowing. The only certainty is that, in addition, he did construct one triumphal arch. The records of the Royal Academy in London show that in 1793 a perspective elevation of a triumphal arch to be erected by Cameron in the Crimea was exhibited by J. S. (?L) Bond.[2] Unfortunately neither the print itself nor any details of the arch, nor where it stood can be traced.

A period of twelve months was a short time to prepare everything for an imperial tour on such a grand scale, and three years were far too few for Potemkin's scheme for his new provinces to materialise, but during 1786 everyone concerned with the project worked with a will, and finally it went according to plan, if not without a little improvisation here and there.

The imagination of Europe was caught by the 'Potemkin villages' on this tour, and the phrase is still loosely used to describe something altogether bogus. Yet this does not seem to be strictly correct. Western historians see only paste-board villages created by Potemkin in order to deceive the Empress; in view of the close relationship between Catherine and Potemkin it seems much more probable that they were working in collusion in this matter. Potemkin's real aim seemed to be to produce what in modern parlance might be called a 'mock-up' of the scene as it would be in the future. The 'villages'—and it is a pity that one can do no more than speculate as to whether Cameron played any part in their construction—were placed on the banks of the Dnieper:

At greater or less distant intervals, the banks of the river displayed pretty insulated dwellings and well-built villages, the extent of which would lead the beholder to expect a numerous population, and their exterior seemed to bespeak the opulence and comforts of the inhabitants. Many of these private houses and villages had but just been built. It has even been asserted that the most distant buildings were unfinished, and had merely a front. They were so disposed with respect to the soil, as to form picturesque points of view, and for the space of three hundred miles the shores of the Dnieper were set out in the form of English parks. As the population of the country was insufficient to give animation to the landscape, peasants had been sent for from several parts of the empire; they were successively removed from one spot to the other (frequently in the night) to give the roads where the Empress was to pass the next day, that bustle and animation which else they would often have wanted.[3]

Not all the spectators were deceived. The Prince de Ligne wrote of 'towns without streets, streets without houses, and houses without roofs, doors or windows'. But he added:

I made several excursions without the Empress, I discovered many things with which even Russians are unacquainted; superb establishments in their infancy; growing manufactures; villages with regular streets, surrounded with trees, and irrigated by rivulets.

This goes to the heart of the matter, that the great design was there. The imperial progress succeeded in attracting attention both at home and abroad to this large and undeveloped part of the empire, and there is little doubt that the Empress did 'give encouragement to, and revive by her presence, every branch of agriculture, industry and administration'. The Empress made her progress down the Dnieper, as far as the cataracts, in a magnificent galley, one of fifty, all with rooms 'hung with Chinese silk and furnished with sofas . . . arranged with much art and taste', indicating again, perhaps, the hand of Cameron. According to plan she went overland to Cherson, a flourishing port and dockyard with nothing paste-board about it.

17   Engraving of a portrait of Paul I given by the Empress
Marie Feodorovna to Sir Home Popham of the Royal Navy
and a print of the empress herself.

18 The Temple of Friendship in the grounds of Pavlovsk, built in 1780.

19   Façade of Pavlovsk Palace designed by Cameron, 1782-5.

20   The Italian Hall, the rotunda in the centre of
Pavlovsk Palace.

21 The Grecian Hall, lined by free-standing verde
antiquo columns, with its superb stucco ceiling.

22. The Great Hall at Kedleston, designed by Robert Adam

23   The Colonnade of Apollo and the Pavilion of the
Three Graces in the grounds of Pavlovsk.

24   Portrait of Alexander I by Sir Thomas Lawrence.
reproduced by Gracious Permission of H.M. The Queen

The peninsula of the Crimea was, of course, the culmination and climax of the whole excursion. That the Empress should actually take up her residence in the palace of the khans at Bakhtchisarai was no mean symbol of sovereignty. Potemkin stage-managed her entrance well; hardly had she crossed into the Crimea than she was surrounded by Tartar cavalry, performing 'various evolutions for the amusement of the Empress'. Catherine thoroughly enjoyed the spectacle. She described it to Grimm in a letter:

Baktchi-sarai. 21 May 1787.
It was a wonderful scene, thus preceded, surrounded and followed, we entered Baktchi-sarai, in an open carriage containing eight people, and we went straight to the palace of the Khans,—there we were installed between the minarets and mosques where they call, pray, sing and turn around five times in the twenty-four hours. We hear all this from our windows, and as today is the Feast of Constantine and Helen we attend mass in a courtyard where a tent has been erected for the purpose. Oh! What a remarkable entertainment to be stopping in this place!

The Empress was certainly under the spell of the East. It is to be hoped that Cameron was at hand to receive her thanks for the part he had played in the rehabilitation of the palace.

It is difficult to discover if the Empress and Potemkin were deliberately provocative in their attitude towards Turkey and actually hoped to goad her into a declaration of war, with the prospect of a speedy victory, or if they considered her to be too pusillanimous to resist their further demands, but it looks as though there had been some sort of miscalculation. In August Turkey sent an ultimatum which Russia could not accept, and the ensuing war dragged on for four long years. The treaty of Yassy which ended it in December 1791 was advantageous to Russia; it confirmed the previous treaty of 1774 and the possession of the Crimea, and extended the western frontier to the Dniester. The policy of the Empress had been so far successful; if not Constantinople, she had yet gained much for her empire. But she had lost Potemkin; he died, worn out at the age of fifty-two, on 15 October 1791.

X

Death of the Empress

On his return from the Crimea in 1787, Charles Cameron for the first time saw Russia at war; but it was not war that reduced his personal world to ruins. Incredible as it may seem, when he went back to Pavlovsk, he discovered that he was no longer architect-in-chief there; he had been superseded, and, unkindest cut of all, by his assistant Vincenzo Brenna.

Catherine had left the Grand Duke Paul and his wife in St Petersburg while she went to the Crimea, and at Pavlovsk they had not wasted their time. They had first met the young designer Brenna, then aged thirty, when they were travelling in Italy, and Paul persuaded him to come to Russia to work for him at his other palace of Gatchina, and from there Brenna went to Pavlovsk to work under Cameron. While Cameron was away and Brenna found himself in charge, he did not keep faithfully to his master's plans, but continued to work in his own much heavier style.

It must have been a sad homecoming for Cameron, although Brenna had not yet achieved the final humiliation, the lengthening of the service wings of the palace, which did so much to alter Cameron's original design. Brenna had, however, accepted the Grand Duchess's views on the Louis XVI style: lamps, modelled on one in the Petit Trianon, hung from some of the ceilings, and the French furniture adorned the new halls. By one of the vagaries of fortune, this turned out in the end to have been an inspired purchase; owing to the destruction of so much of the property belonging to Marie-Antoinette and the aristocracy of France during the French Revolution, the collection which the Grand Duchess Marie-Feodorovna brought back to Russia with her in 1782 remained until the last war the finest collection of Louis XVI furniture in Europe; then, unfortunately, it was dispersed and destroyed by the German army during their occupation of Pavlovsk in 1941.

Cameron could hardly struggle against the tide. He was still the architect in charge at Tsarskoe Selo; he had his own small 'grace and favour' house in the palace grounds where he and his wife lived simply and unostentatiously. He evidently settled down there in 1788 and got to work on his unfinished church of St Sophia—so named in 1779 in the early days of the Empress's dreams of Constantinople—to be completed, by a strange irony, during the harsh reality of the Turkish war. Some of the unlettered villagers even believed at this time that it was a replica of Constantinople's Hagia Sophia, but naturally it was nothing of the sort; it was a modest building in the Palladian manner, with low domes and a columned portico. The Empress herself, in a letter to Grimm (4 September 1794) described the beauties of the interior: ten tall columns, each of a single block of granite, were she said, 'superb', and she explained that the granite, red and black, had been quarried from an island in Lake Ladoga.

That conscientious English traveller, Dr Granville, also praised the church, but without realising who had designed it:

> A very handsome and imposing church, with a hexastyle portico of great beauty, bearing the name of St Sophia appeared in view in the more distant horizon. It is the work of Quarenghi; I need not say more in its praise.

Confusion may have arisen in the tourist's mind from the fact that, by the end of the eighteenth century, another most magnificent palace had arisen at Tsarskoe Selo, the Alexander Palace, built by Catherine for her grandson Alexander, and the Alexander Palace was indubitably the work of Quarenghi during the years 1792–96. There may have been confusion from the very start, because in the letter to Grimm of 4 September 1794 in which Catherine described the church of St Sophia she also made a painstaking catalogue of Cameron's work at Tsarskoe Selo:

> The church of St Sophia is in the village of Sophia, behind the garden of Tsarskoe Selo; it was built by the architect Kameron, nephew of Miss Jenny Cameron: he was brought up at Rome in the household of the Pretender . . . Kameron also built the Colonnade at Tsarskoe Selo, the Bath beside it and the ramp, these are all buildings distinguished by their strength and elegance. The grand staircase of the Colonnade is also by him.

In the year 1790, when the sound of enemy guns was heard in St Petersburg, the Empress for the first time during her reign did not go to Tsarskoe Selo for the summer; it would have been too dangerous, too open to the Swedish menace, and she remained in her fortified capital. When the war was nearly over, in the summer of 1791, the old routine began again and Catherine returned to Tsarskoe Selo. She was now sixty-two and still remarkably fit, except that she had grown very stout, and was glad to make use of the Pente Douce—the ramp—instead of the Grand Staircase, to come down to the garden from the Cameron Gallery (the 'Colonnade') where she spent a great deal of her time. She enjoyed the beautiful views of the park which she could get from it; in fact on 6 June 1791 she wrote to Grimm asking him to invite the French artist Hubert Robert, to come and paint them:

> He could find scenes to paint, for Tsarskoe Selo is one mass of lovely view-points, of the most beautiful vistas you could imagine, and the colonnade alone could provide a good supply of them.

This letter was written 'at 7 o'clock in the morning, on the colonnade, on the left side'; three days earlier, on 3 June, she had written another letter to Grimm explaining to him that she had to sit on the left side of the colonnade because that side was sheltered from the wind, adding, 'you have no idea what Tsarskoe Selo is like when the weather is fine and warm'.

Catherine never lost her youthful energy nor her mental powers, so the end, when it came suddenly five years later, was a shock to all her entourage. On 5 November (O.S.) 1796, the Empress suffered a stroke from which she never regained consciousness and within two days she was dead. It was rumoured that she had disinherited her son in favour of her grandson Alexander. This would have been possible under Russian law but, if such had been her intention, she had taken no steps to carry it out. So it was that at last the Grand Duke Paul, at the age of forty-two, succeeded her as Emperor.

Paul I at once made it clear that he intended to reverse all his mother's policies. If he could, he would have erased her memory: he did his best by his extraordinary action when he insisted on exhuming the coffin of his father, Peter III, from his grave in the Alexander Nevsky Monastery and arranging a joint funeral, so that the Empress and her murdered husband could lie together in the traditional burial place of the Czars in the Cathedral in the Fortress of St Peter and St Paul in St Petersburg. He immediately replaced the old Imperial Guard at the Winter Palace with men from his own palace of Gatchina, in the Gatchina uniform, and he tried to impose a Prussian discipline on his people. The Empress Catherine's friends quickly disappeared from the Court, and it is not surprising that, three weeks after his accession, the new Czar decided to dismiss Charles Cameron from his post at Tsarskoe Selo, and not only to dismiss him but to take from him his 'grace and favour' house. Moreover Paul actually closed the whole palace and would allow no member of the imperial family to live at Tsarskoe Selo[1]:

> The palace was shut up, the great park and the pleasure grounds neglected at the Emperor's orders—so keen was he on obliterating every landmark cherished by his mother.

Cameron's fall was complete and utter. He had lost the royal patronage, he had lost his work and he had lost his home, and financially he may have been in a very insecure position. In 1798[2] he was reduced to selling some of the valuable books from his library to the painter Argounov. He certainly died penniless, which seems to have been an occupational risk for the imperial architects: Rastrelli returned to Italy and died a beggar, Brenna in the end absconded from Russia and died in poverty in Dresden.

Possibly, when his fortunes were at such a low ebb, Cameron may have toyed with the idea of returning to England. Loukomski states that he actually went back, presumably for a holiday, but the *Soviet Encyclopaedia* emphatically denies that he did any such thing: 'Cameron was dismissed by Paul I, but did not leave Russia which he considered as a second homeland'. Cameron had kept up his links with England—recent research has proved that his drawing-paper came from Whatman[3]—and it seems improbable that he would have chosen to visit London, where he must have known that his reception would be chilly. Five years earlier, in 1791, he had been blackballed when his name was put forward for honorary membership of the recently formed Architects' Club; at least this was the occasion when a founder member, Samuel Pepys Cockerell, (father of the more famous Charles Robert Cockerell) wrote his important letter[4] to Henry Holland on 20 November 1791:

I have amended the rules for the admission of Honorary Members. I have stopt at Cameron to reconsider it. It is true he was bred with Ware, and has travelled for Improvement, published some incorrect (as I am told) measures of Antiquities correcting the correct Desgodetz and upon some dispute with his *Father* respecting these Plates, laid him in the Fleet where he languished many years and where he could have died if the Rioters in 1780 had not liberated him. There are some stories, too, about Ware's daughter that incline me to wish his name suspended for the present, altho' Cameron is in distinguished employ in another country. When I met Sandby ten days ago and he mentioned the subject, he particularly wished we might have only men of moral character and high reputation. . . .

Troubles did not come singly to Cameron after the death of his royal patron. Dr Granville tells a sad story about Cameron submitting an unsuccessful design in the competition for plans for the building of the Cathedral of Our Lady of Kazan in St Petersburg (actually begun in 1801). The story may have been told to him by Adam Menelaws (another Scots architect working in Russia) with a certain amount of partizan feelings for a fellow Scot.

(Cameron) presented designs which I was assured by an architect now living in that capital, were superior to those of the Russian artist. Be that as it may, the recommendation of Count Strogonoff, on whose estates it is said the latter was born a serf, prevailed with the Emperor Paul, and the construction of this great temple was entrusted to Voronykhin.

Voronykhin was the architect whom Paul was employing to work with Brenna at Pavlovsk.

Suggestions have been made that Cameron, when he was so much out of favour at Court, went off to the provinces and worked there, and although several plans for country houses, attributed to Cameron, do exist, it is possible that they never left the drawing-board. The period immediately after the death of the Empress would hardly appear to have been suitable for building on any grand scale. The glories of the reign of Catherine II were matched by her extravagance, and paid for in paper currency. As well as worrying over the financial problems, the subjects of Paul I had reason to be alarmed by the instability of the new Czar and his wavering foreign policy. At first he joined Austria and England in their struggle against France, sending troops to Italy under General Suvorov, but when Napoleon became First Consul, Paul made a separate peace and supported him, even to the extent of planning an invasion of India. At home he published *ukase* after *ukase*, and showed every sign of becoming a tyrant, some thought a madman, as his actions became more and more incalculable.

That Cameron should reappear at Pavlovsk in the last year of Paul's reign seems, in the circumstances, more extraordinary than his disappearance four years earlier. Nevertheless all the authorities agree that it was in 1800 that Cameron went back—perhaps at the request of the Empress Marie-Feodorovna—to erect the last of his garden pavilions there. He had, in 1780, been responsible for the Temple of Friendship with its Doric columns, and by 1783 he had built the Colonnade of Apollo, open and circular in form, with a bronze copy of the Apollo Belvedere in the centre. Now in 1800 came the beautiful little Pavilion of the Three Graces (Plate 23). Taleporovski confirms the date for the building of this pavilion, mentioning the existence of a sketch for it signed with Cameron's initial and the date, 'C—1800'. Both Taleporovski and the *Soviet Encyclopaedia* credit Cameron with the construction near Pavlovsk of 'Alexander's Cottage' built by the Empress as a summer residence for her grandson Alexander. The pavilions in its park are also attributed to Cameron: the Pavilion of the 'Rose Without a Thorn' (the title of a fairy tale written by Catherine for the little Alexander) and the 'Echo' Pavilion. There seems, however, to be no documentary evidence for this.

In most books on the subject Cameron is given the credit for the construction of the gardens at Pavlovsk; yet in his *Encyclopaedia of Gardening* (1850) J. C. Loudon, who was so knowledgeable about the Busch family, makes a statement which should be given due consideration—remembering the extreme pressure of architectural work on Cameron during the years 1780–86. Loudon suggests that none other than 'Capability' Brown provided the plan for these very famous and beautiful gardens, the intermediary being Potemkin's English gardener, Gould. Gould, writes Loudon, was a pupil of Brown and was the 'Brown of Russia':

> He had a character analogous to that of his master; he lived in splendour, kept horses and carriages, and gave occasionally entertainments to the nobility. He returned to England and died in 1816 in his native town—Ormskirk, Lancs . . . (The garden) at Pavlovsk presents the best specimen of the English style in the neighbourhood of the Russian capital. It was begun during the reign of Catherine II in 1780 from a design said to have been furnished by the celebrated Brown, from a description sent to him by Gould.

The charming Pavilion of the Three Graces was the last work that Cameron undertook for the Czar Paul I. Shortly after his accession Paul began to build for himself a new palace in St Petersburg, almost a fortified castle, on the site of the old Summer Palace, which he called the palace of St Michael—the Mikhailovsky—and there on 11 March (O.S.) 1801 he was murdered, strangled with an officer's scarf. Paul's rule had been so bad that it could not fail to arouse a spirit of revolt. The ringleader of the finally successful conspiracy was Count Pahlen (Military Governor of St Petersburg and Governor of the Palace), and apparently Paul's eldest son and heir, the Grand Duke Alexander, was implicated in so far as he agreed to accept the crown after Paul's abdication, having received from the conspirators a promise that no harm would come to the Emperor. Pahlen may never have had any intention of keeping this promise, and the consequent murder made Alexander believe that he had been a party to his father's death; it was said that for the rest of his life he felt himself to be a guilty man.

XI

Last Years

The world was told that the Czar Paul I had died of apoplexy, and his son, aged twenty-four, quietly came to the throne as Alexander I. He was a very different man from his father; he had inherited his mother's fine physique and had developed very liberal opinions; perhaps, if he had not been confronted by Napoleon, he might have instituted extensive reforms.

The part he plays in the Cameron story is kindly; he appreciated the architect, and may have remembered him at work at Tsarskoe Selo when, as a child, he stayed there with his grandmother, the Empress. It would make the story more intelligible if it were possible to say that Cameron was absent from the Court all through the reign of Paul I and was then recalled by Alexander I on his accession; but, in the light of the building of the Pavilion of the Three Graces at Pavlovsk in 1800, this is clearly not so. The reconciliation must have taken place in the lifetime of Paul. Taleporovski, Cameron's Russian biographer and the chief authority on his later years, not only confirmed this but states that, in that same year of 1800, Cameron was allowed to return to Tsarskoe Selo, not to his old home but to the flat where his father-in-law, John Busch, had once lived, 'the flat above the orangery', though this does seem more likely to have happened after Paul's death when Tsarskoe Selo was reopened.

In the year 1802 Alexander I appointed Cameron to the post of Architect-in-Chief to the Admiralty, with a flat in the ill-starred Mikhailovsky Palace. By now Cameron was rather a soured man—not surprisingly—and he accepted the post only after some hard bargaining. His Scottish financial acumen had deserted him during the reign of Paul, but now he made his own terms: he asked for and received a salary of 1,500 roubles a year, and his further request for the 'restoration in full of all the privileges to which twenty-three years' service entitled him' was granted. Then, surely remembering his troubles with Kuechelbecker, the Director of building operations at Pavlovsk, he stipulated that he wished to make his reports only to the Emperor, and in 1807 refused to hand over the annual accounts to anyone else.

All the descriptions of Cameron's life at this period are tinged with condescension; the impression they give is of a doddering old man not really fit for his job, more or less a nominal one given to him by the Czar out of the kindness of his heart. This may be true, for there is little to prove it or to disprove it. But the date of Cameron's birth is always given as *c.* 1740, and the date of his apprenticeship makes it seem more likely to have been later, in 1743, so that in 1802 he would at most have been a man of sixty-two, and was more probably fifty-nine, hardly yet in his dotage, unless he had been stricken by some unrecorded illness. It seems strange also to dismiss the post of Architect-in-Chief to the Admiralty so lightly, when the Czar Alexander was about to join the Third Coalition against France, and particularly when Kronstadt, which commands the mouth of the Neva, was rapidly growing in importance as a naval base. Loukomski states that Cameron began the hospital and barracks there and that 'everything built for the Admiralty at Kronstadt or in the provinces rested with him as chief supervisor'; also that in 1804 he worked on projects for Kronstadt Cathedral—although hitherto he had never been very lucky with his ecclesiastical buildings.

In 1803 Cameron had to leave his work at Kronstadt temporarily because the palace of Pavlovsk had been considerably damaged by fire and he was summoned there to help with the restoration. As well as fire damage he found many changes. The Dowager Empress Marie-Feodorovna had made it her residence and, until the end of her life, she employed architect after architect to add to it according to her taste which was still influenced by the Versailles she had known in 1782. More pavilions—and her husband's mausoleum—were springing up in the grounds, where an Italian, Pietro Gonzago, whom Réau calls 'le génial perspectiviste', was completing the landscape gardening as well as painting some pictures for the upper rooms. Voronykhin, who had defeated Cameron in the competition for designs for the Cathedral of Our Lady of Kazan, was also working at Pavlovsk and it is doubtful if anybody took much notice of the creator of the palace:

> Although all was reconstructed, no doubt under the control of Brenna and the supervision of Quarenghi and Voronykhin, this was not done exactly according to Cameron's original drawings.

When Cameron returned to Kronstadt he found himself in trouble again. In 1805 the Minister for the Navy proposed to the influential Count Strogonov, close friend of the Czar and patron of Voronykhin, that Cameron should be replaced as Architect-in-Chief to the Admiralty by the extremely able Russian architect Adrian Dmitrievich Zakharov, who although twenty years younger than Cameron, predeceased him. Loukomski, who gives this information, gives no account of the reasons for this suggestion, and merely states that 'correspondence' about it went on till 1811, i.e. until Zakharov's death, so it seems as though Cameron succeeded in keeping his post. Without reference to Russian naval records it is impossible to know what was involved in this dispute, but it was precisely in 1806 that Zakharov commenced his rebuilding of the Admiralty at St Petersburg, giving it its present form which so dominates the city. It is possible that Cameron, Architect-in-Chief to the Admiralty, might have resented the fact that he had not been given this commission—rightly it must be admitted, for Cameron's genius did not run to the bold and massive lines required of this building which has a façade a quarter of a mile long.

This, however, is pure supposition, and Cameron may by then have begun to show signs of ill-health and failing powers. Both Loukomski and Taleporovski state that he returned to Pavlovsk in 1811, to do some more work there, the last he would ever do. By the spring of the following year he was dead. The actual date of death is unknown, but it is said that the news was given to the Czar on 16 April (O.S.) when he was at Vilna; two months later, on 24 June, Napoleon crossed the Niemen and invaded Russia. In England, in that same month of June, a brief obituary notice appeared in the *Gentleman's Magazine*: 'At St Petersburg, Charles Cameron, Esq, formerly architect to the court of Russia'. So ended the life of one of Scotland's too little remembered sons.

As Cameron left no fortune, and there appear to have been no children, his widow made arrangements for the sale of his library and other effects. The sale which took place during the month of November was put into the hands of Jean Grabit, 78 Nevsky Perspective, St Petersburg. Only one catalogue has survived, and that is now in Moscow and is most revealing. It extends to 210 pages, but the front page advertisement is typical of Cameron's wide reading and many interests:

> A Catalogue of a Library consisting of precious books on Art, Science, History, etc, in the various Languages of Europe, left after the demise of the late Mr Charles Cameron. Of a collection of pictures of three Schools, engravings framed, and drawings in a folder. Also an assortment of instruments mathematical and astronomical, left after the said demise and that of the late Mr Schroeter (Cameron's assistant); and various other articles, such as porcelain, furniture, etc. The sale of all of which shall take place during November 1812.

November 1812 must have been the least propitious month imaginable for a sale of fine books, pictures and furniture. St Petersburg, it is true, was unscathed by war, but much depressed by the news, first of the heavy losses at the battle of Borodino on 7 September, and then by Napoleon's entry into Moscow a week later. The results of that are well known: Moscow burned, and Napoleon and what was left of his Grand Army, making their way home as best they could in the winter snow, did not recross the Niemen until 14 December.

During that terrible November, the prices obtained at auction by Charles Cameron's effects must have been disappointing. Nevertheless the collection was dispersed without trace, with the exception of one leather-bound book of engravings which did survive. In the Introduction to Loukomski's *Charles Cameron* it is stated that:

A bookplate in one of Cameron's books at Tsarskoe Selo bears what appears to be a somewhat Russianised version of the arms of the Cameron of Lochiel. The motto and supporters are exact; the bar has, however, been incorrectly interpreted.

More recently Mrs Tamara Talbot Rice revealed[1] that the book is now in the Palace-Museum of Pavlovsk, and she goes further into the matter, reproducing the bookplate version of the arms which shows it to be correct, except for the motto, which is misspelt: 'Pro Rige et Patria' instead of 'Pro Rege et Patria', a curiously illiterate mistake for Cameron to have permitted. Mrs Talbot Rice does not comment on that, but gives Cameron no quarter for his use of the coat of arms:

> Its use by Cameron does at any rate suffice to show that Cameron considered himself a follower of Lochiel. However, Cameron must have known that he had appropriated Lochiel's personal coat; even Lochiel's eldest son had no right to use it without including a mark of cadency. Other followers of the clan, and this applies to Charles Cameron, are entitled to no more than the Chief's crest in the form of a badge, that is to say enclosed within a strap and buckle, the strap displaying the motto. Such a crest-badge can only be worn and should not appear on any of a clansman's possessions. Cameron's use of Lochiel's personal coat proves that he intentionally misled the Russians with regard to his origin.

Cameron, then, lived out the lie he had told the Empress on his first coming to Russia. It would be interesting to know how much of the truth he told his wife, or how much she discovered for herself, but few as are the records of Cameron's personal life, there is even less information about her. At least everything seemed cheerful and happy on that summer day in 1784 when she went with her husband to St Petersburg to give a 'grand treat' to the workers newly arrived from Edinburgh. And indeed Cameron's memory has remained revered and untarnished in Russia. He appears to have sown all his wild oats in England, and to have been in his adopted country a model of probity and rectitude, quite an acceptable candidate for the Architects' Club for 'men of moral character and high reputation'.

After the Empress Catherine's death in 1796 the Camerons' life must have been insecure and full of anxiety; but the Emperor Alexander showed great generosity to Mrs Cameron when she became a widow. He gave her an annual pension of 1,500 roubles, which was practically the sum her husband had been earning as Architect to the Admiralty. Four years later, when her health became so bad that her doctor advised her to return to England to live with her family, he not only gave her permission to leave Russia, but agreed to continue her pension thereafter. This promise never had to be implemented: the March issue of the *Gentleman's Magazine*, 1817, published the notice of her death—

At St Petersburgh, Mrs Cameron, relict of the late C. Cameron, Esq, formerly architect to the court of Russia.

This record must have escaped Taleporovski, whose book *Charles Cameron* contains the other details, since he falls into the error of believing that Mrs Cameron had sailed for England in the previous August, taking with her her husband's papers and drawings. This is not so, although by some means they were sent to England. There they might have remained had Tsarskoe Selo not been damaged by fire a few years later; in 1820, in order to repair the damage, the Czar ordered his ambassador in London, Prince Lieven, to acquire them from Cameron's next-of-kin. (There is no hint who this could be, but the Post Office London Directory for 1820 gives the address of one Walter Cameron, Russian merchant, as 10 Copthall Court.) Prince Lieven evidently had no difficulty in finding the relatives since he purchased the 114 drawings, but, less generous than his master, he paid only £105 for them, little more than half the price (£200) which had been asked, and he certainly got a bargain.[2] The eminent Russian architect, V. P. Stassov, was entrusted by the Czar with the restoration of the palace; when he had finished with the drawings they were put into safe custody and are now in the State Museum at the Hermitage.

Alexander I showed himself more enlightened than his parents when he thus insisted that Cameron's rooms must remain precisely as he had designed them, and this policy is being continued today in repairing the war damage of 1941. Cameron's work is unique in the USSR; he had few followers, but the Cameron Gallery and his highly personal interior decoration, so different from the Baroque which had preceded it, opened a little wider Peter the Great's 'window on the west'. Catherine the Great recognised this and appreciated it; it was what she wanted, and during her lifetime Cameron was enabled to work as he wished on lavish and expensive projects in a way that would have been impossible had he remained in England. He probably regretted London little, and might have been surprised could he have known that in 1968, almost two hundred years after his *Baths of the Romans* had been received there with total indifference, many of his drawings would be kindly lent by the Hermitage Museum to grace the walls of an Arts Council Exhibition at 4 St James's Square, not so far from his old home at the 'corner of White Horse Street'.

II
THE ARTIST

XII

The Palladian

Rarely has a modern architect designed a distinguished group of buildings
—and Cameron certainly achieved that—without leaving behind him some
apprentice work by which his development can be judged. But in the case
of Cameron any early buildings of his that may exist are clothed in such
impenetrable anonymity that they elude research; as does his mode of life
during two critical periods, from 1772–1775 and 1776–1779.

These gaps are the more tantalising because they cover the most formative
years, when Cameron, by any reckoning, was in his thirties. It is pleasant
to imagine him wandering around London, examining Robert Adam's
work, and perhaps pausing in St James's Square to look at the Ionic columns
on James 'Athenian' Stuart's recently erected Lichfield House, the first
building in the real Grecian style in London. It is also pleasant to think of
him in Paris in the earlier days, watching the sales of the French edition of the
Baths, one of that band of 'artists and collectors of many nationalities' who
gathered at Mariette's print-shop in the Rue St Jacques, and, perhaps,
discussed Ste-Geneviève, the Neo-classicist Soufflot's new church which
became the famous Pantheon, and his dictum that 'the Greek orders should
be combined with the lightness of Gothic buildings'.

Nothing can be proved, and it is unwise to jump to conclusions about
anything concerning Cameron. For example, it might be supposed that a
promising young architect, living 'next door to Egremont House' would
have found a powerful patron in the young Lord Egremont, but Cameron's
name does not appear among the catalogued papers at Petworth House.
So the only way of discovering how Cameron prepared himself for his
successful career lies in considering first the contacts he is known to have made,
and then the influence of his predecessors and contemporaries as revealed
in the work he left behind him. Cameron was a Palladian follower to the
end, but he was also a man of his time, inevitably influenced by the intellectual
climate of the second half of the eighteenth century.

Cameron himself stated that he 'studied under Ware for some time';
from Isaac Ware, therefore, he must have learned the first elements of his
profession. Ware was essentially a practical man; his *Complete Body of
Architecture* was a complete guide for practical architects, and later, in
Russia, Cameron may have been glad to refer to its chapters on 'Materials

used in building, including marble and porphyry' and 'Decorations for a garden (pavilions, temples)'—not to mention 'the effluential parts of building (wells, sewers, drains, etc)'.

Isaac Ware, although a strict Palladian, was somewhat ambivalent in regard to interior decoration, where he had a lighter, less classical touch than some of his fellow Palladians. Some, indeed, believe that, in 1749, he did not come quite unscathed from his task of building Chester-field House for the 4th Earl of Chesterfield, that 'politician, wit and letter-writer' who was also a connoisseur of French Rococo and insisted on furnishings and decorations in that style. This is not to belittle the work Ware did to extend Palladianism in England. The new edition of *Fabbriche Antiche* was unfinished at his death, but in 1727 he had helped to prepare drawings for engravings in William Kent's *Designs of Inigo Jones*, and as early as 1738 he had published a translation of Palladio's *Quattro Libri*, the first correct edition in English; moreover a villa in Kent which is attributed to him, Foot's Cray Place, is a faithful version of the Villa Capra (Villa Rotonda).

Although Cameron would later adopt Pompeian motifs and modify the classicism of his interior decoration, it is not surprising that, with his training, he should, in 1772, launch *The Baths of the Romans* on the world as a defence of pure Palladianism, even then a little outdated. In his book he declared himself a convinced follower of Palladio and of those

> men of discernment who were not so entirely misled as to prefer the specious appearance of excellence to the real and substantial beauty of the Greek and Roman Architecture, when introduced to them in its proper form; and who have re-established the old and true method of building by unanimously giving to Palladio the first place among the modern architects.

It was from the Villa Capra that Cameron chose the painting he used as the frontispiece of *The Baths of the Romans*, the engraving of a bust of Palladio, a picture which at once set the tone of the book. Whether Cameron visited Vicenza and the Veneto and actually saw the Palladian villas cannot be ascertained, but his copy of Bertotti Scamozzi's *Forestiere della Città di Vicenza* (1761—a first edition) now in the Glasgow University Library and inscribed 'Charles Cameron' in his own hand, perhaps a relic of Walter Cameron's dispersal of his son's collection, had on its cover a small ink sketch (since removed and mounted) which is 'very certainly the work of Cameron and shows the detail of one bay of the Basilica at Vicenza, which Bertotti Scamozzi engraved for his work'.[1] (Plates 5 and 6)

Scamozzi, in that first edition of his book, did not include Cameron in the list he gave of British architects he had met in Vicenza: Robert Adam, Brettingham, Chambers and Wynn. In any case Cameron in 1761 could have been only twenty-one, probably younger, and there was obviously no personal contact between them at that time, and perhaps never. Scamozzi, however, was familiar with the 1772 French edition of *The Baths of the Romans*; in 1785 he referred to that book and its author in glowing terms in his own Italian reprinting of Lord Burlington's *Fabbriche, Le Terme dei Romani*. He refers to Cameron as 'il celebre Sig. Architetto Carlo cameron', and 'il erudito Sig. Cameron', and calls the *Baths* 'questa pregiatissima Opera'—greater praise than Cameron received in his own country at any time.

Cameron made his aims for *The Baths of the Romans* clear in his *Proposals* for publishing it by subscription, which he issued in 1770[2]:

Piccadilly, March 20th, 1770.

P R O P O S A L S

For Publishing by

S U B S C R I P T I O N,

In ONE VOLUME FOLIO,

Upon a Fine IMPERIAL PAPER, Elegantly engraved on EIGHTY COPPER-PLATES,

By CHARLES CAMERON, Architect,

THE

THERMÆ of THE ROMAN EMPERORS.

The BATHS of the ROMANS (especially those built under the emperors) are considered by cotemporary writers as the most magnificent of their works. The great remains of them at ROME have induced the admirers of antient architecture to examine the structure of them with care and attention.

Some copies from the studies of PALLADIO relating to these Baths were engraved and published under the direction of the late Lord BURLINGTON; but that valuable work becoming very scarce, ISAAC WARE, Esquire, Secretary to the Board of Works, formed a plan of reprinting it: Mr. CHARLES CAMERON (who studied under him for some time) made it his business, during his residence at ROME, to complete the designs Mr. WARE left imperfect at his death.

These designs, therefore, he proposes giving to the public, verified, and corrected; with their measures from his own observations; adding the antique ceilings, paintings, and other ornaments belonging to the THERMÆ.

He likewise proposes to accompany this work with views, elevations, and sections, from accurate drawings taken on the spot, representing the present state of these buildings, and shewing the authorities upon which the restorations of PALLADIO are founded.

The principal Baths treated of are those of AGRIPPA, TITUS, ANTONIUS CARACALA, DIOCLESIAN and CONSTANTINE: the author, in his researches into the history and structure of these Baths, has been greatly assisted by the permission given him, by the late Pope; to dig in such places as he might think conducive to his general plan; by these means he has gained such information as to enable him, in his dissertation upon this subject, to throw great light upon several passages which have hitherto been considered as very obscure. The whole will be illustrated by references to the best authors who have treated upon this subject, and compared with the present remains.

As nothing will be omitted that can contribute to render this work as complete as possible, Mr. CAMERON hopes, that the credit arising to him from it will compensate for the labour and expence he has been at in the prosecution of such an arduous undertaking.

••

The price of SUBSCRIPTION will be FOUR GUINEAS, as mentioned in the advertisement of March 25, 1770; and before, in March 1767. This work is so nearly completed, as to enable him to promise it to the Subscribers early next Winter, according to his Proposals.

Specimens may be seen at Mr. ROBSON, New Bond-Street; Mr. PAYNE, the Mews-Gate; Mr. WESLEY, Holborne; Mr. PRINCE, Oxford; Messrs. MERRELL, Cambridge; and at the AUTHOR, next door but one to Egremont-house, Piccadilly; where subscriptions are taken in.

The title page of the *Baths of the Romans* when it was at last published made the
same point more briefly:

THE

BATHS

OF THE

ROMANS

EXPLAINED AND ILLUSTRATED.

WITH THE RESTORATIONS OF PALLADIO
CORRECTED AND IMPROVED.

TO WHICH IS PREFIXED,
AN INTRODUCTORY PREFACE,
POINTING OUT THE NATURE OF THE WORK.

AND A DISSERTATION
UPON THE STATE OF THE ARTS
DURING THE DIFFERENT PERIODS OF THE ROMAN EMPIRE.

By CHARLES CAMERON, Architect.

LONDON:
PRINTED BY GEORGE SCOTT, CHANCERY LANE:
AND TO BE HAD OF THE AUTHOR, NEXT DOOR TO EGREMONT-HOUSE, PICCADILLY.
M DCC LXXII.

XIII

The Baths of the Romans

Cameron, when writing his book, did keep his reverence for Palladio this side idolatry. He was fully prepared, as he had said on his title page, to 'correct and improve' the restorations of Palladio, and this he does to most purpose in his description of the Baths of Titus which he had himself excavated (or rather re-excavated, since the earlier excavations had fallen into disrepair). Plate VII shows a plan of the Baths with Palladio's measurements, but, in addition, his own plan of the subterranean vaults; Plate VIII then gives the 'Elevation of the Baths of Titus, as restored by Palladio'. In his chapter on the Baths of Caracalla there are fewer plates but the letterpress contains more criticism:

> In this place there is the remains of a stair-case. I cannot imagine the stairs to have been as Palladio has put them, for the crown of the arch is standing. . . . There is but one stair-case. *Query*. Where was the communication to the other side, for the vault between went up to the height of two stories?

In this chapter Cameron also stated that 'not long since there remained in this place a fragment, representing two gladiators, now in the possession of Cardinal Albani', from which it might be inferred that he had obtained an introduction to the old cardinal and had seen his renowned collection of classical antiquities at the Villa Albani. Whether or not Cameron met the cardinal's librarian, J. J. Winckelmann, would depend upon which season of the year he made his trip to Rome because in June, 1768, the unfortunate Winckelmann was murdered in Trieste. It was from Winckelmann's descriptions of the excavations at Pompeii and Herculaneum that students were first accurately informed of the treasures there, and Winckelmann's *History of Ancient Art*, published in 1764, had a great influence on his contemporaries. His famous phrase describing the 'noble simplicity and calm grandeur' of classical art embodied the ideal of the Neo-classicists that Cameron achieved. Cameron must have read his book in a French translation as in his *Introduction* to the *Baths* he quotes from 'the Abbé Wincleman . . . l'Histoire de L'Arts'.

One chapter each in Cameron's own book is given to the Baths of Agrippa, Nero, Titus, Domitian and Trajan, Caracalla, Constantine, and Diocletian; the last 'corrected from the present remains' measures in English feet and inches. These seven chapters are preceded by two preliminary chapters, one on the *Apartments belonging to the Baths* and the other *Of the Baths of the Romans under the Emperors.*

In these two chapters and indeed throughout his whole dissertation on the state of the arts during the different periods of the Roman Empire Cameron quotes from a large number of authorities, Latin, Greek, French and English: Strabo, Tacitus, Pliny, Suetonius, Seneca, Cicero, Lord Burlington, Camden, the Abbé du Bois, not to mention St Jerome and St Gregory and even Theodoric. Sometimes his views on the fall of the Empire seem to echo an old Calvinism, sometimes to foreshadow Gibbon. Sometimes he digresses to discuss subjects of interest to him, but not entirely relevant to his argument. He must have recognised that he had this rather endearing frailty when he wrote:

> In treating upon subjects which engage the attention, we are very apt to be led away by ideas, which, at first sight, seem naturally to arise from the point in question, but which a more mature consideration rejects as foreign to the purpose. For this reason the writer should often put himself in the place of the unconcerned man, that he may keep as clear as possible of those prejudices and partialities, which notwithstanding all his endeavours will sometimes get possession of him.

The text occupies fewer pages in the volume than the plates, of which there are seventy-five, as well as twenty-five within the text as chapter headings and endings, and these vary slightly in the French version which otherwise is identical. Only three prints bear Cameron's signature: Plate XXI, 'Capital and Cornice of the Doric Order, from the Baths of Dioclesian', signed 'C. Cameron, Archtus, fecit'; Plate XXIII, 'Corinthian Order from Dioclesian's Baths', signed 'Carolus Cameron, Archtus' and also 'B. Mayor. Pictor, fecit', which suggests that Cameron had here induced an engraver friend to help him. (Barnaby Mayor, artist and engraver, was a member of the Society of Artists and died in 1774.) Then Plate LXXI, 'Triton from the ceiling at Adrian's Villa' has the curious unfinished signature 'C. CAM' Other prints are taken from the *Fabbriche Antiche* and there are also some by Piranesi, whose publications had inspired many to undertake archaeological research. (Plate 25)

The excavations of the Baths of Titus not only yielded corrections for Palladio; their ceilings provided Cameron with no less than eleven plates to illustrate *The Baths of the Romans*, many of them very delicate work. Cameron seemed to be obsessed by ceilings; some of those he reproduces in his book have little if any connection with the Imperial, or any other Baths. Such are the plates of the ceiling from Hadrian's Villa, and the three plates of a 'ceiling imitated from the Villa Madama' (Plate 26). The latter are of special interest, illustrating as they do a factor in Cameron's development, the influence of Raphael.

The Villa Madama, outside the city walls of Rome, was designed and begun in the sixteenth century (about 1516) for Cardinal Giuliana di Medici, later Pope Clement VII. The original design was by Raphael, and it is thought that he directed the work on the frescoes and stucco decorations until his death in 1520. The villa had an enormous influence on other Renaissance villas built in Italy and its decorative motifs, inspired as they were by those found on the remains of imperial buildings, held a special appeal for Charles Bameron; the motifs of the ceilings were to reappear in his later work in Russia.

XIV

Robert Adam

Today the 'Adam style' is a term so widely used that it is apt to be loosely applied to any artist's work which may happen to resemble it, so it would be wise to consider—as far as that is possible in the absence of documentation —if Charles Cameron independently developed his own style, or if indeed his art is derivative.

Because Robert Adam was the older man, well established in practice in London when Cameron was still in his teens, it is all too easy to dismiss Cameron as just another follower and imitator of Adam. The similarities are there, it is true, but the manner in which Cameron dealt with the very different problems he had to solve in Russia is the measure of his genius.

It seems unlikely that the two men ever met, since class barriers were almost insuperable at that time. Robert Adam, it may be remembered, on his first arrival in Rome was most anxious that it should not be known that he was an architect: 'If I am known in Rome to be an architect, if I am seen drawing or with a pencil in my hand, I cannot enter into genteel company who will not admit an artist'.[1] Cameron, on the other hand, had no social pretensions; he appears in *Hayward's List of British Artists in Rome in 1768* as 'Mr Cameron—architect'. It has also been pointed out that in the list of subscribers to Woolfe & Gandon's Vol. V of *Vitruvius Britannicus* he appears again as 'Charles Cameron, architect' without the 'Esquire' permitted to James Paine, John Taylor, etc, 'probably because he was known to be of humble birth'.[2]

If this precluded a meeting between them when Adam had himself been accepted in 'genteel company', there was nothing apparently to prevent Cameron from studying Adam's early work in London. But to him this would not have appeared quite as revolutionary as it did to his fellow citizens. Like Robert Adam he had travelled abroad; he had learnt, at first hand, of the new trends on the Continent, and knew about the amazing discoveries at Herculaneum and Pompeii; he, too, admired the work of Clérisseau, and Clérisseau is one of the most elegant of architectural artists. There was, in fact, at this time a common pool of knowledge, available to all who sought it.

It is unfortunate that none of Cameron's drawings made at the peak of his career are in Britain, though some early ones are in the Sir John Soane

Museum and British Museum (Plate 4). For comparison to be made it is necessary to visit the State Hermitage Museum in Leningrad, which now has the largest collection of his designs and sketches. Some of these designs, such as the elevations for an 'unidentified country house', have an even greater delicacy of drawing than Adam's and some sketches, in pen and ink with colour wash, have a distinctive beauty of their own. His ceilings, too, have all a recognisable individuality, but here both men owe more than a little to William Kent.

Robert Adam and Charles Cameron excelled as interior decorators with their similar, but not identical styles:

> Cameron used elongated lines, columns surmounted by small capitals, and arch-like garlands of Pompeian frescoes as neither Adam nor Clérisseau would have done.[3]

When the styles tend to become identical, as in the Grecian Hall at Pavlovsk, which resembles so closely Adam's Great Hall at Kedleston, there is always the possibility that the Empress Catherine had commanded that it should be so. Yet here again both men had equal access to James Paine's *Plans, Elevations and Sections of Noblemen's and Gentlemen's Houses* published in 1767, which contained his original plan for the central block at Kedleston (before the building was taken over by Adam) and it was Paine who had 'the brilliant idea of placing in sequence the antique basilica hall and a Pantheon-like circular saloon'.[4]

In fact the two men never lose their individual touch. The French are right in thinking that 'the style is the man'; their roles were not interchangeable. The mind boggles at the thought of Adam confronted with Catherine the Great and the riches of Russia, or of Cameron as London's most fashionable architect.

Both Robert Adam and Charles Cameron were, of course, Scotsmen, but of very different types. Adam was brilliantly successful, pushing his way to the top. Cameron had the mind of a scholar, with perhaps a more thorough knowledge of classical architecture obtained at first hand. He chose to spend days alone investigating and measuring a site in Rome, while Adam, who perceived very quickly what was likely to be of use to him, was content to be guided by Clérisseau. Cameron was receptive to the new ideas being brought back from ancient Greece, whereas Robert Adam had not a good word to say about James 'Athenian' Stuart. There was also the important and basic difference that Adam was no self-confessed Palladian.

They had, however, one thing very definitely in common—their national spirit of independence; once their designs had been accepted they would brook no interference from their patrons that might disturb the harmony and unity of the whole. Cameron at Tsarskoe Selo designed everything himself to suit the individual rooms, from chandeliers and fireplaces to the smallest keys and door-knobs; Adam did as much in England, giving his attention as much to Spitalfields silk hangings for the walls of Syon House as to the carpets on the floors. It is a testimony to their strength of character and artistic integrity that each could so impose his will: Cameron working in Russia for a single patron—Catherine the Great—and Adam working at home for the nobility and gentry of Great Britain.

XV

Tsarskoe Selo – Interior Decoration

At Tsarskoe Selo in four years Cameron devised and decorated three suites of rooms for the Empress Catherine in Rastrelli's old palace. They were known as the First Apartment (1780–82), the Fourth Apartment (1781–84) and the Fifth Apartment (1782–84). There were no Second or Third Apartments.

The First Apartment, built at the north end of the west facade consisted of eight rooms: Blue Drawing Room, Chinese Cabinet, Ante-Room, Green Dining Room, Bedroom, Music Room and two service rooms, and was, of necessity, simpler in style than Cameron's later work because, being on trial, he had to use the materials he had at hand.

Loukomski states that the ante-room was the first to be finished; it is in severely classical style, very plain, the walls broken by carved wooden pilasters, made to resemble marble, with plaster capitals, and frieze. Like the different, but still conventional Blue Drawing Room, it was not characteristic of Cameron's later work. The Chinese Cabinet and Music Room showed signs of what was to come, but his imaginative genius in this first essay revealed itself most surely in the richly decorated Green Dining Room and in the pistachio green Bedroom, and both owe little either to Robert Adam or to Clérisseau. Indeed A. E. Richardson in an article in the *Architectural Review* (Vol. 39. 1916) wrote:

Charm and delicacy, together with profound archaeological knowledge, distinguish Cameron's dining-room at Tsarskoe, and for technique and execution and appropriate furnishing it stands unrivalled. The rich modellings on the lower parts of the walls are, however, carried to excess; they detract from, rather than add to the beauty of the inlaid doors, the exquisite fire-place and rich ceiling. But the modelling has the merit of boldness, which is not apparent in a good deal of the work of the Brothers Adam.

Here was the influence of Pompeii. Cameron modelled the stucco 'Antique figures' on the walls in far higher relief than was ever employed by the Adam brothers, and placed medallions, also of stucco, on the panels, one of his more constant motifs (Plate 11). In his notes in the catalogue of the Cameron Exhibition (1967) Mr A. A. Tait makes the interesting suggestion that Cameron may have gained some inspiration for this room from the Villa Albani in Rome 'where arabesques were used to frame Antique sculptures in a similar manner'.

Cameron was a meticulous artist, and the number of alternative designs he was prepared to submit to his patron can be judged from the three sketches for the Green Dining Room in the Hermitage Museum.

Each shows what variations were considered before the final stage was reached; the lowering of the height of the ceiling, for example, the changes made in the 'Antique figures' and the reduction in the space given to arabesques.

The Bedroom was the most original conception in this first suite. The walls were soft pistachio green with white stucco decorations, and slender green and white porcelain columns (some used to define the bed recess) gave it an air of great delicacy and grace. The idea was repeated by Cameron in the magnificent bedroom he later constructed for the Empress herself in the Fifth Apartment (Plates 10 and 30).

The construction of the Fourth Apartment (containing the Arabesque Room, Lyons Drawing-Room, Chinese Hall and Rotunda) required greater ingenuity than that of the First, because it was sited close to Rastrelli's Great Hall and over the void where Rastrelli's stair-case had been. And, such are the problems that must be solved by interior decorators of old buildings, the designs had to incorporate Rastrelli's windows, an integral part of his façade.

Cameron dealt with the situation by first converting two of Rastrelli's five antechambers to the Great Hall into his Arabesque Room and Lyons Drawing-Room, a not unworthy link between the old and the new. Loukomski describes the Arabesque as 'a mixture of styles characteristic of the epoch'. Sprays effectively framed the existing windows, and the wall panels again showed Pompeian influence, but it was on a grander scale than anything in the First Apartment (Plate 27).

Unfortunately the Fourth and Fifth Apartments suffered severely from damage during the Second World War, and now all the rooms are in process of restoration and cannot be described at first hand. But in the case of the Arabesque Room and Lyons Drawing-Room what the public saw from the mid-nineteenth century onwards was not what Cameron designed. In 1823, after partial destruction by fire, they had been redecorated, and Loukomski, writing in 1935,[1] states that the Arabesque Room was again repainted in 1863, while in the Lyons Drawing-Room only the 'original framework, Cornice and floor' remained; the chimney-piece had been entirely reconstructed. Loukomski's descriptions must be respected because, as Architect and Curator of the Palace, he had access not only to Cameron's sketches, but to his models of the rooms which were preserved at Tsarskoe Selo until 1942. Probably the present repair work will restore the Fourth and Fifth Apartments to their pristine glory, and fortunately it is still possible to gain factual details about their original state and Cameron's intentions from his own and contemporary descriptions.

The Arabesque Room led into the sumptuous Lyons Drawing-Room. Cameron had discovered that the wealth of Russia was now his for the asking; here he used gilt bronze in place of stucco, and lapis-lazuli was inlaid in doors, walls, tables and candelabra supports. The Lyons Drawing-Room got its name from the beautiful yellow patterned Lyons silk used for wall panels and upholstery. Above the stone-framed, ornate bronze door were three paintings representing 'two apparitions and an adoration' by Ivan Scotti, who had painted the panels in the Music Room of the First Apartment. Above this was a frieze in Italian Renaissance style, with garlanded cattle and sheep, and the bronze heads of bulls. Below was a magnificent parquet floor, in which were incorporated fifty different kinds of wood, plus a mother-of-pearl inlay.

It is tempting to try to trace the influence of Clérisseau on these rooms since the Empress had a very large collection of his drawings, and specifically stated that she had shown them to Cameron to help him in his work on her new rooms. Mr A. A. Tait sees the Arabesque Room as 'the most French of Cameron's designs' and suggests that here 'the tradition that Cameron was a follower, if not plagiarizer of Clérisseau is given strength'. Nevertheless not one room designed by Cameron is a replica of anything devised by Clérisseau, and it seems not unreasonable to consider that Cameron had little need to study the Imperial collection of Clérisseau's drawings when he had already in Rome absorbed and assimilated the teaching of the master himself.

The large and handsome Chinese Hall, adjacent to the Lyons Drawing Room and covering most of the space previously occupied by Rastrelli's staircase, would seem to have sprung straight from Cameron's 'fertile brain'. It may be noted that Mrs Talbot Rice[2] found in that Hall 'many strange things' such as Greek motifs which, she considered, revealed Cameron as a precursor of the Romantics rather than a follower of Robert Adam. Cameron was, in fact, a man cognisant of, and reflecting contemporary architectural ideas in England, France and Italy.

This Chinese Hall might have been the idea of the Empress, because the craze for *chinoiserie* which swept across western Europe in the eighteenth century had already reached Russia. This curious art form was by no means an imitation of actual Chinese buildings and artifacts; it was a purely western development, based on seventeenth-century travellers' tales of the fabulous East, when European artists gave expression to their vision of an idealised China, and its peak was in the mid-eighteenth century. In England the most famous exponent of the art was Sir William Chambers, who had actually visited China. His *Designs for Chinese Buildings* was published in 1757 and in 1762 he built for the Princess Dowager of Wales the well-known pagoda in Kew Gardens. Cameron must have read the book and studied the subject, for one of his first tasks at Tsarskoe Selo was to design additions to the 'Chinese Village' already in the park. He actually designed an eight-storied pagoda and some pavilions, but only a few of these were built. The Chinese Hall in the palace was quite another matter; it was completed as planned and was extremely successful, stamped with his own personality.

With Rastrelli's staircase gone another had to be provided, and in order to fit the smaller space Cameron evolved a somewhat attenuated one, leading up to the Cupola Room, or Rotunda, whence it was possible to pass into the Chinese Hall on the left, or go straight on to the Fifth Apartment that led in turn to the terrace and the Agate Pavilion and Cameron Gallery. This small Rotunda was entered from a landing and as the name implies, was circular in shape and had a dome which Mr A. A. Tait sees as coming 'straight from the North Italian Baroque of Vittone'.

The most important development in Cameron's art shown in the Fourth and Fifth Apartments was his use of bronze. He was lucky on his arrival in St Petersburg to find the Imperial bronze foundries already in existence. The Empress Catherine had established them in 1765 but as they had concentrated mainly on the making of firearms, Cameron re-equipped the buildings under an able French director and personally supervised the work done for him there. Nothing was too big or too small: fire grates with sphinxes, griffons, lions, tigers and dragons; fire-dogs decorated with gilt bronze eagles; the bull heads for the frieze; door-handles, locks and keys; chandeliers, candle-brackets and bronze decorated lamps; all these were cast and chased after Cameron's designs, and under his own eye. He expected perfection, and he got it. He was at this time able to employ the best men for all the decorative work. Charlemagne was the specialist in carved woodwork, and there were four cabinet makers of whom one, Brullo, specialised in gilding. The wrought iron work for ornamental screens and fire-guards was forged by Basseli. Cameron was also lucky to find glass, porcelain, and silks all in production in St Petersburg. Peter the Great's glass factories had been transferred from Moscow in the mid-eighteenth century; the Imperial Porcelain Factory had been expanded by Catherine and early in its history was producing work of a high standard. The manu-facture of silk fabrics had been introduced into Russia by the Empress Elizabeth, and by Cameron's time they were said to be 'indistinguishable from the French'. So when he came to work on the Fifth Apartment Cameron was at no loss for materials and craftsmen.

The Fifth Apartment was the most important of all, since it was Her Imperial Majesty's private suite. It contained six small rooms: the Silver Cabinet, the Blue Room (or 'Tabatière'), the Bedroom, the Mirror Room, the Boudoir and the Raphael Room. The Silver Cabinet, entered from the Chinese Hall, was used by the Empress for private audiences and official correspondence. Loukomski suggests that 'the name might be derived from the character of the furniture, which has since disappeared'[3]—like most of the original decoration.

The Blue Room, known as the 'Snuff-Box' because its small size and delicate colouring and decoration recalled just such an *objet d'art*, may well have inspired Miss Alison Kelly to call Cameron's style 'Fabergé Adam'. The room was panelled in opalescent glass festooned, in light Pompeian style, with bronze garlands covered with leaf gold in various tints, superimposed bronze eagles and, of course, medallions. On either side of the doors were slender columns of moulded blue glass, with small bronze bases and capitals, reminiscent of the First Apartment. The furniture was of mahogany or rosewood, upholstered in slightly tinted white silk, and one side of the room was filled by one large couch. Reminiscent also of the First Apartment was Cameron's use once again of plain glass over felt to produce a shimmering effect, this time from choice, there being now no need to economise. It was a decorative practice also employed by Robert Adam at Northumberland House, where he placed gilt lead and coloured metal foil under plate glass; an example of this in the Victoria and Albert Museum is dismissed by one art historian as being 'vulgar in the extreme'[4], something which has not been said of Cameron's version.

The Empress must have approved the novel style of the bedroom in the First Apartment because glass columns reappear in the magnificent—though small and comfortable—bedroom Cameron made for her next to the Blue Room, with which it had much in common. But in the bedroom the colouring was lilac and mauve instead of blue, and a lighter effect was obtained by placing mirrors between the columns to give long perspectives, and by using Wedgwood medallions instead of bronze.

This use of Wedgwood was an innovation, and twenty-two or so of these plaques were used in this bedroom. The well-known 'Dancing Hours', designed by Flaxman, was set at the top of the over-mantel mirrors; above the wall panels were more plaques, the 'Bacchanalian Figures', and others were over the windows; in the chimney-piece were inset fifteen smaller medallions (Plate 30).

It would be easy to explain the presence of these English plaques as a routine order sent over by Josiah Wedgwood from his 'Etruria' factory. In 1770 he had supplied the Empress with the famous 'Husk' dinner service, and, four years later, with the 'Frog' service, and being an excellent public relations man, he let the world know immediately of such satisfactory imperial patronage. But, and here lies the mystery, it seems that Josiah Wedgwood himself had no knowledge of these later deliveries to St Petersburg. Miss Alison Kelly, in her authoritative book *Decorative Wedgwood*, published in 1965, stated that 'there are no records in the archives of the firm of correspondence either with Cameron or the Empress about these transactions. Recently when studying the Wedgwood account at Drummonds Bank, however, Miss Kelly discovered entries showing that Mr Peter Capper, an English merchant in St Petersburg, paid Wedgwood over £1000 between 10 March 1789 and 13 September 1790, a sum so large that Miss Kelly believes it represents the Tsarskoe Selo commission, suggesting that Cameron placed the order with Capper.

In her book Miss Kelly recorded an interesting correspondence which Wedgwood had with Capper, when Wedgwood did not seem anxious to accept his order, even although he had said that it was 'for an artist employed at Court':

> I observe your friend orders tablets considerably larger than they are asked for in this country, and I wish it were consistent with his design to have some of them less. They would come very expensive so large if I had the models by me, but that being the case with a few only, the time and expense for modelling the remainder of these sizes would be too great to think of.

Wedgwood's provisional estimate was for 'little, if any, less than £300'; nevertheless Capper ordered four large plaques (27 ins × 12 ins) and a large number of smaller ones. As the Drummonds Bank account reveals one payment of precisely £300, another of £500, and three others for lesser sums, it does appear that the route to Russia travelled by the Wedgwood plaques has at last been discovered.

The Raphael Room, a small reception room opposite the bedroom, naturally reflected that 'Raphaelism' about which the Empress had once written to Grimm, and it was probably suggested by her. She already owned Raphael's *Virgin and Child with St Joseph*, part of the Crozat collection purchased in Paris in 1772. Six years later, by her command, Reiffenstein in Rome arranged with Unterberger to have Raphael's frescoes in the Vatican copied on canvas and sent to St Petersburg. In 1783, the very moment when Cameron was engaged on this Fifth Apartment at Tsarskoe Selo, Quarenghi was starting work on the gallery which was to receive them, an extension to the Hermitage and a replica of the famous Loggia in the Vatican. The copies of the frescoes did not arrive in Russia until 1785, so Cameron's design for his Raphael Room must have been based on his own memories of Rome, including both the Vatican and the Villa Madama. The room contained copies of Raphael's paintings and the style was Renaissance rather than Pompeian, with oil painted pilasters and frieze. Christopher Marsden, indeed, in his *Palmyra of the North*, wrote that 'the little Raphael Room, with its semi-gothic arched panels and screen' showed Cameron's 'adaptability to the contemporary search for novelty in style'. At any rate it showed his versatility (Plate 27).

The Mirror Room, a small writing-room next to the bedroom was less akin to it than to the Raphael Room. The 'semi-gothic arched panels' reappeared, but painted porcelain pilasters framed long slender mirrors as in the bedroom. Loukomski suggests that the design here was influenced by Clérisseau.

The Fifth Apartment was now finished; with the Mirror Room Cameron reached the outer wall of the old palace and by cutting a door through it, he gave Catherine direct access to his new terrace garden and to the projected Agate Pavilion and colonnade, later to be known as the Cameron Gallery.

XVI

The Agate Pavilion and Cameron Gallery

Cameron was, for Catherine the Great, the perfect architect; everything that the Empress wanted he provided. When she asked for a new style in interior decoration he gave her those rooms of the First Apartment that 'people rushed to see', because, as she said, 'they had never before seen anything like them'. Then came the handsome rooms of the Fourth Apartment, and the complete privacy, for which she craved, of the Fifth. Now he was about to make a superb extension of these private apartments by building out from them a terrace, prolonged by a covered Ionic colonnade—the Cameron Gallery. The baths building, the Agate Pavilion, was quite close to the entrance to the Gallery, set back to the left and on the same level.

There has been some confusion in nomenclature here, because the name Agate Pavilion is often bestowed on the whole building, whereas it applies more accurately only to the first floor, which consisted of six public rooms, including the sumptuous Agate, or Great Hall, and the Jasper Room. The baths were on the ground floor and here again there is more confusion, because the whole complex gained the generic name of the Cold Bath, although that was only a small part of the whole. Further confusion arises also in the case of the Cameron Gallery: obviously Cameron would not have given his own name to the Gallery, which originally was known as the Colonnade. The Empress referred to it as such in her letter to Grimm on 4 September 1794 when she mentioned Cameron's buildings: 'the Colonnade at Tsarskoe Selo, the Bath beside it and the ramp', adding, very truly, 'these are all buildings distinguished by their strength and elegance'.

Once Catherine stepped out from the Mirror Room on to the terrace she literally left the old Baroque palace behind her, and saw only the 'calm grandeur' of the new gallery, its white Ionic columns reflecting in some degree the classic beauty of the Erechtheum on the Acropolis, as much a novelty to her subjects as the style of the interior decoration had been. The path she followed from the private apartments along the terrace ran between colourful flower beds, the 'terraced garden' she had specified, while the Gallery fulfilled not only her demand for 'the same view from her windows

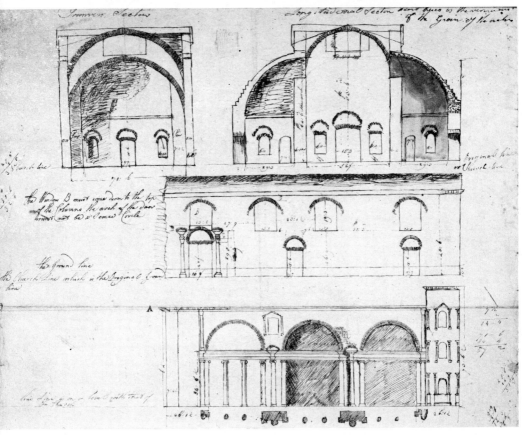

25   Classical sources: Doric capital engraved by Cameron for his book together
with some of the preparatory drawings he made of the Baths of Diocletian.

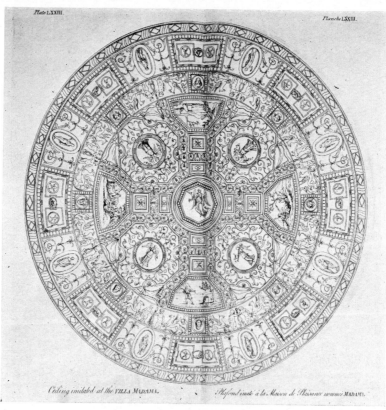

Ceiling imitated at the VILLA MADAMA.   Plafond imité à la Maison de Plaisance nommée MADAMA.

26   Renaissance influence: *The Villa Madama*, attributed to
Clérisseau. Plate of ceiling design in the Villa Madama
from *The Baths of the Romans*.

27 Cameron's Arabesque Room in the Fourth Apartment, the Raphael
Room and the ceiling from Catherine's Bedroom in the Fifth Apartment, Tsarskoe Selo, before the Second World War.

28 & 29 Elevation of the fireplace wall of the Great Hall, Agate

skoe Selo, and the ceiling as it was finally painted and stuccoed.

30 The fireplace in Catherine's bedroom in the Fifth
Apartment, Tsarskoe Selo, before the Second World
War, showing the Wedgwood plaques and the bronze
decorations mounted over glass panels.

31   Elevation and section of the staircase well in the Agate
Pavilion at Tsarskoe Selo.

32 Section through an unidentified country house designed
by Cameron. Tsarskoe Selo in the twentieth century:
war damage in the Green Dining Room and tourists in
the Cameron Gallery.

as from the balcony', but gave her so many 'lovely view-points' that she wished Hubert Robert to come and paint them.

The Gallery was cunningly contrived to provide comfort as well as elegance and vistas. Cameron remembered that the northern sun does not shine every day, and that the wind could whistle through the columns, so he enclosed the central passage with a protective glazing. There the Empress could sit in inclement weather and, on occasion, dine in state. Ample illumination was provided by those large candelabra which Cameron designed so well, but here they were made of carved wood, not of marble and bronze, in order to match the furniture which was of wood, 'simple but imposing' and very decorative on account of its fine quality. The open sides of the Colonnade, however, Cameron furnished with 'small folding arm-chairs in wrought iron, after the Greek style'.

This emphasis on the Greek style is interesting. Cameron had written in his *Baths of the Romans* of the 'real and substantial beauty of the Grecian and Roman Architecture', and here he was a little ahead of his time. Although James 'Athenian' Stuart, in collaboration with Nicholas Revett, had published the first volume of the *Antiquities of Athens* in 1762, and about the same time had built Lichfield House in St James's Square using the Erechtheum Ionic order, the vogue for the Greek orders and proportions rather than the Roman did not flourish in England until the nineteenth century. Cameron must have studied Greek architecture to some purpose because in 1780, the year after his arrival at St Petersburg, he built in the gardens at Pavlovsk the circular Temple of Friendship, using a pure Greek order for his Doric column and entablature which thus appeared for the first time in Russia.

The stucco-pillared front of the Agate Pavilion, with its medallions and niches filled with statues, was also classical, but here Roman influence predominated in the low Pantheon-like dome. The Vestibule Hall led directly to the most important of the first floor rooms, the Agate, or Great Hall, which effectively set the tone for the others. In the decoration of them all Cameron was aiming at polychrome effects with rich materials; jasper and agate, for example, in the Jasper Room, where for the walls he used green jasper, for the columns red agate with gilt bronze capitals, and throughout there were large ornamental vases of porphyry, jasper, malachite and lapis-lazuli.

The Great Hall itself was severely classical with a colour scheme of pink and white marble. The window wall was divided into three equal bays by free-standing agate columns with bronze Corinthian capitals, which supported the barrel-vault roof; the windows were flanked by square-headed niches containing statues and surmounted by large sculptured marble medallions. Mr A. A. Tait comments:

the use of the free-standing column, the division of the wall into three bays, and the sculpture-filled niches, are reminiscent of Robert Adam's work in the Ante-room at Syon.

The design for the fireplace wall (Plate 28) was similar. The chimney pieces were made of white marble and red agate; over each mantel was a large bas-relief panel with an agate and bronze frieze, and on either side of the fireplaces were marble goddesses holding aloft bronze candlesticks. Loukomski states that these statues were 'remarkable for the delicacy of their execution and classical grace' and were executed by Rachette from designs by Cameron. This seems most probable; Rachette was a French sculptor who had arrived at St Petersburg in 1779—the same year as Cameron—to work at the Imperial Porcelain Factory. As he was the same age as Cameron and likewise an admirer of Clérisseau the two men must have had much in common, and Rachette may have been responsible for some at least of the marble medallions and bas-reliefs. Others were the work of the Russian sculptor Martos who had been trained by Gillet, the French Director of the School of Sculpture at the St Petersburg Academy of Fine Arts. Miss Alison Kelly has not been able to confirm that Wedgwood plaques and medallions were used in the Agate Pavilion, though old photographs and returning travellers suggest that they were; nor can she find any evidence for Loukomski's statement that Flaxman actually worked at Tsarskoe Selo for Cameron, although she finds one chimney-piece 'strikingly Flaxmanian'.

A staircase, with steps of red agate and a bronze hand-rail, led down from the Agate Pavilion to the Cold Bath on the ground floor. Being his own architect now, and freed from the restrictions that conditions at the old palace had imposed on him, Cameron was able to build a more impressive staircase here than the one he had designed to replace Rastrelli's, and to roof the well with a shallow dome (Plate 31).

The Cold Bath was actually a large complex based on the Roman model with certain Russian adaptations. The bather passed from the dressing-room into a 'Frigidarium' where there was a swimming-pool, then into a comfortable room with divans and an open fire and a warm bath; beyond that lay the hot bath and rest rooms, and finally the Massage Room.[1] Of this latter Mr A. A. Tait notes that 'the simple chaste decoration is typical of that found in this suite of rooms. A taste for asymmetry is displayed in the perverse balancing of unlike urns of porphyry which flank the window. The cornice which runs round the room is a distant variation upon the classic metopes and triglyphs pattern.'

From their very purpose it would seem that these rooms would have to be more severe in style than the others, but the nature of the site may also have influenced Cameron. As the building advanced it became more and more evident that, because of damp, marble and stone must be used instead of wood and stucco, and according to Taleporovski the erection of the stone vaulting produced many problems. Possibly this was the determining factor that made Cameron decide to bring his own workmen and master-masons over from Scotland. To them Taleporovski pays a generous tribute, saying that what they taught their Russian work-mates did much to 'advance the skill and technique of Russian builders at the beginning of the nineteenth century'. One of the baths was of white marble, copied from a Roman model, with a stone canopy supported by four columns, and taps of gilded bronze.

When increasing age made it difficult for Catherine to use the staircase leading from the end of the Gallery to the gardens, Cameron devised a ramp for her with such skill that it appears to be an integral part of his building, giving no hint of being a later addition. The Pente Douce, as it became known, led down from the terrace at a central point opposite to the entrance to the Agate Pavilion. Owing to the sloping nature of the site chosen for his extension of the palace, Cameron had to raise the terrace and gallery to the level of the Mirror Room by setting them on a base of rusticated arches. Now he showed his artistry, his ability to make his work blend with its environment, when he set his ramp on large but gradually diminishing arches to match those which already formed the lower storey of the terrace, Gallery and Agate Pavilion. But in order to make the ramp more decorative and important—and it was very conspicuous at this particular point—Cameron placed masks in the Italian Renaissance manner on every key-stone. Loukom-ski's opinion was that the balustrade of the ramp was 'inspired by the villas of Italian Cinque-cento, as seen at the Villa Lante at Bagnaia, or at Caprarola'. This was Cameron's last addition to the Catherine Palace.

XVII

Pavlovsk

Pavlovsk, the first palace or dwelling-house known to have been created by Cameron, is very much what was to be expected from such a devoted follower of Palladio. Attention is focussed on the central building, which is a cube surmounted by a low Pantheon-like dome; this, however, breaks with Palladian tradition by being supported on a drum encircled by sixty-four slender pillars—an elegant addition. Unfortunately the two semi-circular arcaded flanking wings were extended later by Brenna, an enlargement of Cameron's elliptical courtyard which threw it out of proportion with the building. The façade was simple in conception: the ground floor is unadorned and acts as a pedestal for four pairs of white Corinthian pillars (two stories high, the frieze above them being at roof level) that stand out well against the pale ochre colouring of the building. The garden façade has a somewhat similar portico at first floor level, but with six Corinthian pillars and pediment.

Mr George Heard Hamilton[1] considers that at Pavlovsk Cameron's debt to Palladio can be traced to a wood-cut in the *Quattro Libri*, the design for the unfinished Villa Trissino at Meledo. Certainly the two have much in common: both were designed to be built on a hill-top—even if not a very big one—and Palladio for the first time here developed what has been described as a

> new spatial dimension: upward as well as back and to the centre. Palladio not only used the rise in the land to elevate this building, but also a huge masonry substructure to create a sequence of platforms.[2]

Although Cameron did not use platforms at Pavlovsk he did gain height by making his ground floor no more than a base for his pillars which, as in the Villa Trissino, rise to roof level, to be surmounted by the dome. The resemblance is close, but it must be remembered that by a strange chance the Villa Trissino—with no more than half a wing built—has had a formative influence all over the world. Cameron was not alone in using the plan for the Villa Trissino as a model; Jefferson, in the U.S.A. made a closer replica when he designed the University of Virginia buildings at Charlottesville.

Pavlovsk, however, is not on the scale of the University of Virginia; in fact Mr Heard Hamilton, in his previously quoted book, levels the criticism ainst it that:

It was Cameron's largest commission but it must be said the whole is too small in scale to be truly palatial; however exquisite the Palladian details it is obviously the work of a decorator rather than an architect.

But in her *Concise History of Russian Art* Mrs Tamara Talbot Rice makes the interesting point that it is this very lack of size, 'the unpretentiousness of Pavlovsk which endears the place to the Russians'.

The interior of Pavlovsk followed the Palladian plan closely but not rigidly. In the centre of his rectangular block Cameron placed a rotunda (immediately under the dome) which became the Italian Hall. On one side of it was the Grecian Hall, on the other the vestibule and staircase; to the right was the Hall of War leading to the Grand Duke's apartments, to the left the Hall of Peace led to those of the Grand Duchess; the library, picture gallery and service rooms were in the wings.

Because Cameron left Pavlovsk in 1786 before it was completed, and because so much of the work was carried on by Brenna, it is difficult to distinguish the rooms directly attributable to Cameron. Grabar, in his *History of Russian Art* allows him only the Grecian Hall, the Italian Hall and the Dressing-Room, while Kourbatov, in his *Pavlovsk*, adds the Hall of Peace. From the style of decoration this seems reasonable, and leaves little doubt that the Hall of War, as completed, was Brenna's.

Of all the Halls at Pavlovsk the Grecian Hall is the most important and the most magnificent. It is rectangular in shape with walls of imitation white marble; several feet away from them free-standing verde-antiquo Corinthian columns, about six feet apart, line the room, looking very handsome against the light colouring of the walls. At intervals between the columns stand large vases of porphyry and alabaster on pedestals as in the Agate Pavilion, and in the walls are niches holding marble statues 'in the antique style'. The ceiling is highly ornamental, the central coffering being surrounded by stucco richly decorated with Greek motifs, the whole supported by Corinthian columns. Everything is in harmony, including the furnishing of Greek-style stools. The Grecian Hall can easily stand comparison with Adam's hall at Kedleston (Plates 21 and 22), and would indeed be hard to equal.

In the adjacent Italian Hall, a rotunda beneath the central dome of the building, Cameron was influenced not only by the Pantheon but by the Roman Baths. Loukomski gives the best description of it:

It is circular, with a cupola lighted from above, and has deep niches all round. It is decorated with reliefs brought from Italy and placed on mauve and white artificial marble walls. A frieze decorated with eagles and garlands is surmounted by a gallery of which the windows and the oriels are separated by caryatids supporting the dome.

Cameron founded no school, nor had he any immediate followers, but the Russian architect Ivan Starov used the Italian Hall to some extent as a model for the Central Hall in the Taurida Palace in St Petersburg (1783–89) which he built for the Empress to give to Potemkin. This Hall was actually known as the 'Pantheon'.

Pavlovsk marks the summit of Cameron's professional career; no commissions on any extensive scale again came his way. It is true that many of his plans exist for country houses, some in great detail showing 'even the morticed joists' of a roof, but the houses themselves have remained 'unidentified', and Loukomski's claims that Cameron designed the palace of Batourin for Count Razoumovsky is difficult to substantiate.

The charming Pavilion of the Three Graces, built in the grounds of Pavlovsk in 1800, was Cameron's swan-song but showed no diminution of his imaginative genius. He was not responsible for the Three Graces themselves (a somewhat uninspired marble group by Triskorin) but his Pavilion, with its colonnaded portico, in which they stand, is perfect in style and proportion—a purely Greek building with Ionic columns, reminiscent, like his Gallery, of the Erechtheum.

Cameron's curiously isolated position makes it difficult to estimate the extent of his influence on the many Grecian-style buildings which were erected during the reign of Czar Alexander I. He was a pioneer in Russia and an architect whose place in the history of European Neo-classicism should not be forgotten. What the USSR thinks of Charles Cameron is revealed in the loving care and skill with which their craftsmen are repairing the terrible war damage of 1941. Like a phoenix Cameron's work is rising from the ashes, a tribute to his genius.

Notes

CHAPTER I
1 All the Empress's letters quoted (translated from the French) are from *Sbornik* (Imperatorskoe Russkoe Istoricheskoe Obschestvo Vol. 23).

CHAPTER II
1 Guildhall Library. M.S. 4329/17.
2 Middlesex Land Register. M.D.R. 1743. St George's, Hanover Square 1/131.
3 Westminster Public Library. Rate Books 1740–65. (Parish of St George's, Hanover Square).
4 Middlesex Land Register. M.D.R. 1776. St George's, Hanover Square 2/16.
5 Guildhall Library. M.S. 4329/19.
6 Westminster Public Library. Poll book for Westminster By-Election November 1749. (St George's, Hanover Square).
7 Survey of London XXXII p. 451 (St James's, Westminster).
8 One of the supplementary volumes by Woolfe & Gandon. A list of subscribers appears in the book.
9 R.I.B.A. Correspondence Files (quoted by D. Stroud in *Henry Holland, his life and architecture*). Also p. 69.
10 Register House, Edinburgh. GD/18/4683 (Penicuik Papers).

CHAPTER III
1 W. T. Whitley, *Artists and Their Friends in England* 1700–1799 (London 1928).
2 Tamara Talbot Rice, *Charles Cameron*, Arts Council Exhibition Catalogue, 1967.

CHAPTER IV
1 This mansion was demolished in 1928, but engravings of it appear in Ware's *Complete Body of Architecture*.
2 Quoted from a record in the Middlesex Record Office by Tamara Talbot Rice in *Charles Cameron*, Arts Council Exhibition Catalogue 1967.
3 Westminster Public Library. Rate Book, May 1775 (c. 350). St George's, Hanover Square.
4 Public Record Office. King's Bench Entry Book of Judgements, Hilary Term 1775, Fol 2 Index 9645.
5 Public Record Office. King's Bench Entry Book of Judgements, Easter Term 1775, Index 9772.
6 Public Record Office. King's Bench Entry Book of Judgements, Trinity Term 1776, Fol 20 Index 9646.
7 Middlesex Land Register. M.D.R. 1776. St George's, Hanover Square 2/16.
8 Middlesex Land Register. M.D.R. 1776. St George's, Hanover Square 3/2.
9 Middlesex Land Register. M.D.R. 1775. St George's, Hanover Square 4/275.
10 Public Record Office. Common Pleas Plea Roll. Michaelmas Term 1776, m 410 (CP 40/3727).
11 Corporation of London Archives, Guildhall.
12 Not translated into Russian until 1939.

CHAPTER V
1 *Voltaire: Correspondence* 1772, Vol. 82, 1963, ed. Theodore Besterman.
2 J. C. Loudon, *Encyclopaedia of Gardening*, London 1850.
3 J. C. Loudon, op. cit.
4 Quoted by Tamara Talbot Rice in *Charles Cameron*, Arts Council Exhibition Catalogue, 1967.
5 A. B. Granville, *St Petersburg: A Journal of Travels To and From that Capital*, London 1828.

CHAPTER VI
[1] George Heard Hamilton, *Art and Architecture of Russia*, Pelican History of Art, 1954.

CHAPTER VII
[1] Tamara Talbot Rice was fortunate enough to come across all the details in documents in various hands in Edinburgh. *Charles Cameron*, Arts Council Exhibition Catalogue, 1967.
[2] V. N. Taleporovski, *Charles Cameron*, Moscow 1939.
[3] Public Record Office. Russian State Papers, FO 65 (quoted by Tamara Talbot Rice in *Charles Cameron*, Arts Council Exhibition Catalogue 1967).
[4] Georges Loukomski, *Charles Cameron*, London 1943.
[5] George Heard Hamilton, op. cit.

CHAPTER VIII
[1] V. N. Taleporovski, *Charles Cameron*, Moscow 1939.
[2] According to Loukomski before the war.
[3] *Journal of RIBA*, August 1936.
[4] V. N. Taleporovski, *Charles Cameron*, Moscow 1939.
[5] *Journal of R.I.B.A.*, August 1936.
[6] *Ibid.*

CHAPTER IX
[1] *Memoirs of the Life of Prince Potemkin*, London 1812 (translated from the German).
[2] Possibly John Linnell Bond (1764–1837). Exhibited RA 1782–1814.
[3] *Memoirs of the Life of Prince Potemkin*, London 1812

CHAPTER X
[1] E. M. Almedingen, *The Emperor Alexander I*, London 1964.
[2] Georges Loukomski, *Charles Cameron*, London 1943.
[3] Supplement to *Charles Cameron*, Arts Council Exhibition Catalogue, 1967.
[4] R.I.B.A. Library Correspondence Files.

CHAPTER XI
[1] Tamara Talbot Rice, *Charles Cameron*, Arts Council Exhibition Catalogue, 1967.
[2] Georges Loukomski, *Charles Cameron*, London 1943.

CHAPTER XII
[1] A. A. Tait, *Charles Cameron*, Arts Council Exhibition Catalogue, 1967.
[2] Clerk of Penicuik Papers, GD 18/4683. H.M. General Register House, Edinburgh.

CHAPTER XIV
[1] J. Fleming, *Robert Adam and His Circle*, London 1962.
[2] Tamara Talbot Rice, *Charles Cameron*, Arts Council Exhibition Catalogue, 1967.
[3] Georges Loukomski, *Charles Cameron*, London 1943.
[4] J. Fleming, H. Honour, N. Pevsner, *Penguin Dictionary of Architecture*, London 1966.

CHAPTER XV
[1] *Connoisseur*, Vol. 95, 1935.
[2] Mrs Talbot Rice in a BBC Radio Three discussion on the Charles Cameron Arts Council Exhibition with Berthold Lubetkin, 31 December 1967.
[3] *Connoisseur*, Vol. 96, 1936.
[4] Peter Murray in *A History of English Architecture*, Kidson, Murray and Thompson, Pelican 1965.

CHAPTER XVI
[1] V. N. Taleporovski, *Charles Cameron*, Moscow 1939.

CHAPTER XVII
[1] *Art and Architecture of Russia*, Pelican History of Art 1954.
[2] James S. Ackerman, *Palladio*, Pelican 1966.

Bibliography

The Baths of the Romans Charles Cameron (London 1772, 1775)
Charles Cameron V. N. Taleporovski (Moscow 1939)
Charles Cameron Georges Loukomski (London 1943)
Charles Cameron c. 1740–1812 T. Talbot Rice and A. A. Tait, Cameron Exhibition Catalogue
  (Arts Council of Great Britain, 1967)

NEWSPAPERS AND PERIODICALS

Newspaper cuttings from the *Scotsman* relating to Miss Jenny Cameron (Edinburgh 1907.
  National Library of Scotland. Blk 687)
Articles on Charles Cameron by Georges Loukomski:
  Apollo August and September 1942
  Architectural Review January 1943
  Country Life 17 June, 1939
  Connoisseur April, July, November 1935
  Journal of R.I.B.A. August 1936
Architectural Review. Vols. 38 (1915) and 39 (1916) 'Classical Architecture in Russia' by A. E.
  Richardson, F.R.I.B.A.
Gentleman's Magazine 1772, 1812, 1817.

GENERAL

Architecture in Britain 1530–1830 John Summerson (Pelican History of Art, 1953)
Dictionary of National Biography
Dictionary of Architects
Biographical Dictionary of English Architects 1660–1840 H. M. Colvin (Murray 1954)
Soviet Encyclopaedia (Bol'shaya Sovetskaya Entsiklopediya)
History of Russia Bernard Pares (Cape 1926)
A Concise History of Russian Art Tamara Talbot Rice (Thames & Hudson 1963)
The Penguin Dictionary of Architecture (Penguin 1966)
A History of English Architecture Kidson, Murray & Thompson (Pelican 1965)
Biographical Dictionary of Painters & Engravers M. Bryan 1893
Dictionary of Booksellers & Printers 1772–75 Plomer Bushnell Dix 1932
Sbornik (Imperatorskoe Russkoe Istoricheskoe Obschestvo. Vol. 23)
Catherine the Great Ian Grey (Hodder & Stoughton 1961)
Catherine the Great E. M. Almedingen (Hutchinson 1963)
So Dark a Stream E. M. Almedingen (Hutchinson 1959)
The Emperor Alexander I I. M. Almedingen (Bodley Head 1964)
Palladio James S. Ackerman (Pelican 1966)

CHAPTER I

Memoirs of the Margravine of Anspach (London 1826)
History of the Camerons Alex. Mackenzie (Aberdeen 1884)
History of the Rebellion 1745–46 R. Chambers (Edinburgh 1869)
Jacobite Memories R. Chambers (Edinburgh 1834)
Life & Adventures of Prince Charles Edward Stuart I W. Drummond Norie
Lyon in Mourning I (Scottish History Society 1895)

CHAPTER II

MSS in Guidhall Library (Court Minute Books & Apprentice Binding Books of the Carpenters' Company) 4329/17 & 4329/19
4337/4
MSS in Corporation of London Archives at Guidhall: Lists of Prisoners in the Fleet
MSS at Greater London Record Office (Middlesex Land Register):
  MDR 1743. St George's Hanover Square 1/131
  MDR 1776. St George's Hanover Square 2/16
MSS in the Archives of the Westminster City Libraries:
  Records of St George's, Hanover Square
  Rate Books 1740–1765
  Poll-book for Westminster By-Election November 1749
MSS Will of Isaac Ware (Probate Registry, Somerset House)
MSS Hayward's List of British Artists in Rome in 1768 (British Museum)
Clerk of Penicuik Papers. GD. 18/4683 H.M. General Register House, Edinburgh
History of the Carpenters' Company E. B. Jupp (2nd ed. 1887)
Berkeley Square to Bond Street B. H. Johnson (Murray 1952)
The Universal Director "Mr Mortimer" (London 1763)
Survey of London XXXII (St James's, Westminster, North of Piccadilly)
Complete Body of Architecture Isaac Ware (London 1756)
Henry Holland, his life and architecture. D. Stroud (Country Life 1966)
Dictionary of Contributors to Society of Artists of Great Britain 1760–91
Free Society of Artists 1761–83 Algernon Graves. (London 1907)
Free Society of Artists, A Descriptive List illustrating Catalogues in the possession of Basil Jupp
  (1871) (Victoria & Albert Museum G9)
Artists & Their Friends in England 1700–1799 W. T. Whitley (London 1928)
Scots in Italy in the Eighteenth Century Basil Skinner (Edinburgh 1966)
Robert Adam & His Circle John Fleming (Murray 1962)

CHAPTER III

John Stuart, 3rd Earl of Bute J. A. Lovat-Fraser (Cambridge 1912)

CHAPTER IV

MSS Archives of the Westminster City Libraries:
  St George's Hanover Square. Rate book May 1775 (C350)

MSS Public Record Office. King's Bench Entry Book of Judgements:
  Hilary Term 1775 (Index 9645)
  Easter Term 1775 (Index 9772)
  Trinity Term 1776 (Index 9646. TT 1776 fo 20)
  Common Pleas Plea Roll, C.P. 40/3727 (Michaelmas Term 1776 m 410)
  Abstract Book of Commitments 29 August 1776: Prison 10/22, and 31 August 1780 Prison 10/137
MSS Greater London Record Office. (Middlesex Land Register)
  M.D.R. 1776 St George's Hanover Square 2/16
         1776 St George's Hanover Square 3/2
         1775 St George's Hanover Square 4/275
MSS Corporation of London Archives, Guildhall:
  List of Prisoners in the Fleet 28.1.78
  List of Prisoners set at large 1780
Dictionary of Irish Artists I Strickland (Dublin 1913)
Manuel du libraire et de l'amateur du livre J. C. Brunet (Paris 1860)
Nouvelles Archives de l'Art francais 4 series XVII (Paris 1932) (Correspondence of Catherine II
  with Grimm and with Falconet)

CHAPTER V

Correspondence of Jeremy Bentham Vol 2. (ed T. Sprigge. Athlone 1968)
Unpublished Diary of Elizabeth Dimsdale (quoted in Arts Council Exhibition Catalogue, 1967,
  by T. Talbot Rice)
Memoires, Prince de Ligne (Paris 1827–9)
The Hermitage Pierre Descargues (Thames & Hudson 1961)
Voltaire—Correspondence 1772 (Vol 82 1963) ed Theodore Besterman
Capability Brown Dorothy Stroud (Country Life 1951)
Encyclopedia of Gardening J. C. Loudon (London 1850)
St Petersburg A Journal of Travels To and From that Capital. A. B. Granville MD, FRS,
  MRCP. (London 1828)

CHAPTER VI

Art & Architecture of Russia George Heard Hamilton (Pelican History of Art 1954)
Winds of Change Harold Macmillan (Macmillan 1966)

CHAPTER VII

MSS Seafield Papers GD 248/518/6 H.M. General Register House Edinburgh
MSS Public Record Office. F.O. 65. Russian State Papers
Palmyra of the North Christopher Marsden (Faber & Faber 1943)
Memoires, Comte de Ségur (Paris 1825)
Diaries & Correspondence James Harris, 1st Earl of Malmesbury (London 1844)

CHAPTER VIII

Saint-Pétersbourg Louis Réau (Paris 1913)
Journal of R.I.B.A. August 1936. Article by G. Loukomski
Memoirs of Marie-Antoinette Madame Campan (London 1823)

CHAPTER IX

Memoirs of the Life of Prince Potemkin, translated from the German. (London 1812)

CHAPTER X

R.I.B.A. Library—Correspondence Files

CHAPTER XV

Decorative Wedgwood Alison Kelly (Country Life 1965)
Chinoiserie Hugh Honour (Murray 1961)

Index

N.º 10992.